lines to
.. all the time . . . . . .

~~got~~ to be big sometimes, you know,
you
~~it~~ got to be small,
sometimes
to run ~~you~~ got to crawl

Now I ~~can't~~ be big all the time,
sometimes I ~~it~~ got to crawl ~~small~~,
I mean, when you
and when you see me, really see me ~~out this~~ mean...
it's just when ~~I'm fighting~~ you at war ~~something besides~~ to be nothing at all.

~~stone~~ . . . .
~~stone~~ . . . .

know
~~do~~ you ~~understand~~, ~~stone~~.

Now, I aint good all the time
But I am fightin the clime.
I don't give a goddamn about the dime,
I am fightin the clime.
truly
I am lookin for the inside line...
somebodys
the thing that straightens ~~my~~ spine.

PRINTMAKING TODAY

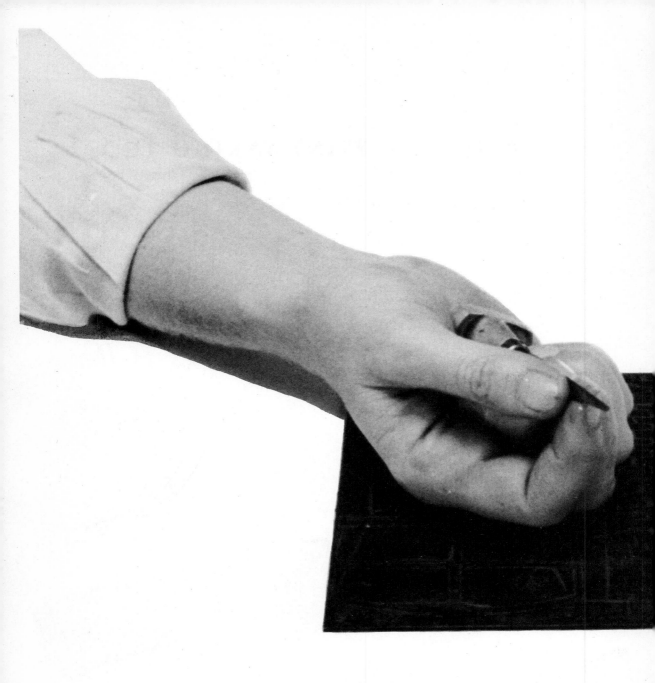

Holt, Rinehart and Winston
New York - Chicago - San Francisco
Toronto - London

PRINTMAKING TODAY

an introduction to the graphic arts

by *Jules Heller*

UNIVERSITY OF SOUTHERN CALIFORNIA

To G. S. H. with love

10 11 12 13 14 15 16 17 18 19

COPYRIGHT © 1958, BY HOLT, RINEHART AND WINSTON, INC.

LIBRARY OF CONGRESS CATALOG NUMBER 58–6295

2057156

PRINTED IN THE UNITED STATES OF AMERICA

ACKNOWLEDGMENTS

IN A TECHNICAL WORK such as this, it is difficult, if not impossible, to isolate and credit primary sources. I am profoundly indebted to many authors, artists, and professional printers—though most of them would not necessarily agree with my particular approaches to the field of printmaking. Consequently, I take full responsibility for whatever errors of omission or commission may be found. Sources and credits for all illustrations, for which I am most grateful, may be found in the list of plates. I am equally grateful to the many artists who submitted prints for inclusion in this book; I wish all of them could have been accommodated in the final version. For many kindnesses rendered, I wish to thank Dr. Viktor Lowenfeld of The Pennsylvania State University, Ray Faulkner of Stanford University, Michael L. Simmons, John Paul Jones, Jakob Zeitlin, William A. Motta, illustrator, and Delmore E. Scott, photographer. To Louis Gross for his excellent photographs of the various processes, and to Gerry Boyd, his model, my sincere appreciation. I am deeply indebted to the Grunwald Graphic Arts Foundation, and especially to Mr. Fred Grunwald for aid and the freedom of his collection. To the University of Southern California my indelible thanks for a research grant in the graphic arts; to my colleagues, and especially to my students during the past decade, many *te deums*.

J. H.

Los Angeles, California
November, 1957

CONTENTS

ILLUSTRATIONS

INTRODUCTION

A SENSITIVE, intelligent art educator preparing for an informal talk on "Printmaking Today" closets himself in his study, picks up his favorite art journal, and settles down to read the lead article, "Renaissance in the Fine Print." After skimming the third paragraph, lips pursed, head nodding almost imperceptibly in a sort of syncopated gait, he seems to swallow with difficulty, clutches the journal in his tensed fists, and stares fixedly at words like "nervously worked lucite surface," "cellocut," and "plaster print." Tossing the periodical across the room, he moves to his desk and writes a letter to a printmaker friend for clarification . . .

Brooks Arnauld, internationally respected print collector, slowly paces the current exhibition of prints in the gallery, searching new talent. The well-groomed, stocky figure pauses before new works of artists already in his possession, analyzing, evaluating, judging their qualities in relation to those in THE COLLECTION. From time to time he writes codelike references on the crisp catalog of the exhibition with a small gold pencil. Suddenly, he stops transfixed before a large print on the wall. Neither his great knowledge of technique nor the handsome catalog aid him in understanding how this work was accomplished. That queasy feeling in the pit of his stomach comes again and again as he finds other prints employing still more unusual techniques. Hurriedly, he leaves the gallery and repairs to his *sanctum sanctorum* to write a letter to a printmaker friend for clarification . . .

With humility, I submit this book about fine prints. I hope it proves useful to art students, professional artists, print collectors, and laymen who desire information, on many levels, about the making of lithographs, woodcuts, etchings, engravings, serigraphs, and related print mediums. On the assumption that the reader will attempt but one medium in the graphic arts before proceeding to another, the book was designed as a series of separate "islands" complete unto themselves.

What is a fine print? It is a multiple-original work of art on paper which comes into direct contact with a stone, plate, wood block, or silk screen that was worked upon by the artist—and which was personally controlled, in many instances, throughout the entire printing of the edition. Reproductions of other works of art, no matter how esthetically pleasing, should not be confused with fine prints. A fine print may be produced lovingly and patiently, or violently and impetuously—dependent upon the "climate" of the printmaker. From a fleeting idea wrested from the complex of human experience, worked through to the final visual image on paper, the print is employed as a medium in its own right. It is utilized by the printmaker for what it alone can accomplish in serving his particular needs. This precious sheet of paper bears the autographic trace of the printmaker on its surface; in his own "handwriting," then, we read the record of his dreams, his hopes, aspirations, play, loves, and fears.

The primary reason for the existence of the print lies in the multiplication of original works of art, despite current practice which arbitrarily limits editions. The print, this multiple-original work of art, can reach potentially a much wider audience than can the unique examples from the fields of painting and sculpture. Many families can live with the same original from the hand of the artist—for quite dissimilar reasons—and all may derive enjoyment, pleasure, good, inspiration, and whatever else may be ascribed to the subjective, personal reactions possible from the visual image. The possibilities inherent in the idea of the print as a democratic medium are still to be realized in the technologically weighted, atomic, and atomistic-minded era of today.

Despite the fact that the fine print is not a mass medium of communication, the audience of the printmaker increases day by day. The feudal-like patronage of the great print collector of the past is giving way to the democratic patronage of many small print collectors of the present. As compared with other works of art that are purchased by the few for many dollars, prints are purchased by the many for few dollars.

More and more colleges and universities are adding printmaking to their curricula. Print societies, clubs, and workshops spring up to meet the needs of the new collectors, the old connoisseurs, the growing body of printmakers. Exhibitions of prints abound in art schools, museums, small independent galleries, and universities, as well as in such unlikely locations as laundromats, theater lobbies, and supermarkets, to name but a few.

Within the past ten years or so, the "face" of printmaking has undergone violent plastic surgery. The small, intimate, black-and-white impression known, collected, and loved since the fifteenth century is being displaced by prints which rival easel paintings in size, color, and importance. New techniques and new materials fuse to produce prints that confuse the old connoisseurs; they can't tell one medium from another any more without a catalog to aid them. The layman is even more bewildered by this dazzling display of technical virtuosity. Art students and professional artists not familiar with these new techniques in the graphic arts are similarly bewitched. All of the innovations in tools, materials, and methods are gathered here in the hope of providing a richer vocabulary, a new point of departure for printmakers now, and in the future.

Many excellent treatises on single aspects of the graphic arts are available; many others have been out of print for so long they are rare and difficult to obtain. Some are rather dogmatic in approach and tend, therefore, to be of questionable value for the alert beginner. Others are too obscure to permit of a successful experience by the uninitiated. Still others suggest certain dualisms, especially in the field of lithography, which destroy the unity of the activity for the individual. (These are the books which claim it takes an "artist" to draw upon the stone, and a "printer" to make the edition.)

Stated in other terms, a thorough search of the literature in the field revealed that there was no one book which treated satisfactorily *all* of the mediums in the graphic arts. In an effort to meet this need, both for his students and others, the author has set out to codify, to explain, and to make clear such technical information as is necessary to produce a print with its own special kind of beauty, whatever the medium selected.

In the field of graphic arts we use the word "print" to encompass any one or all of the many mediums that may be employed by the printmaker. Yet, a brief examination of the illustrations in this volume reveals that each particular medium has a "look" all its own. How, then, can we differentiate between these various approaches to the fine print?

One way of classifying prints is based upon the *method by which they are printed*. There are four separate methods of printmaking: (1) planographic, (2) relief, (3) intaglio, and (4) stencil. The common name for each of these approaches is: (1) lithography, (2) woodcut and wood engraving, (3) etching and engraving, and (4) serigraphy or silk screen printing. Let us examine each of these different processes briefly:

The planographic process—lithography.

Perhaps it is because of the unusual material employed that lithography holds such fascination for artist and layman alike. Or, it may attract others because of its autographic qualities. At any rate, a lithographic drawing is made with a grease pencil upon the surface of a block of limestone; there is no particular requirement about the drawing save that it leave a deposit of grease upon the stone. After chemical treatment with gum arabic and nitric acid, an ink-charged roller is passed over the wet limestone. Ink is accepted by the grease image at the same time as it is repelled by the undrawn areas of the stone. A print is obtained by placing a sheet of damped paper upon the inked stone, which sits on the bed of a lithographic press, and then running the stone, paper, and the necessary backing under the scraping pressure of said press. Lithography, then, is based upon the antipathy between grease and water; it is essentially chemical in nature; it may be considered a surface phenomenon, in that *the image on the stone is neither above nor below the surface being printed.*

The relief process—woodcut.

Though disarmingly simple in technique, the woodcut holds many pitfalls for beginners seeking "easy" solutions to printmaking. Woodcuts are made in a most direct fashion. Using a well-sharpened knife and a few gouges upon a plank of wood, the artist cuts away all those lines and areas not required in the finished print. What remains of the original wood surface, after the image is cut, is inked and printed onto paper. If you examine a rubber stamp or the type on the striking keys of your typewriter, the principle of relief printing should be readily apparent. The woodcut, then, is made with a knife on a piece of plank-grained wood; *the image to be printed stands in relief on the block of wood.* Wood engravings are printed in the same manner as the woodcut; wood engravings, however, are made on specially prepared end-grain blocks of hard wood, are cut with burins and other gravers, demand greater printing pressure, and, puristically speaking, are composed of white lines on a black ground.

The intaglio process—etching.

A later development of the goldsmith's art brought about intaglio printing. *The image or design, in this instance, is engraved or etched so that it is below the surface of a metal plate.* Ink is forced into the grooves or channels, while the surface of the plate is wiped clean. An impression or print is obtained when the plate and a sheet of damped paper are run through a clotheswringer-type press under great pressure. The pressure is sufficient to force the damped paper down into the lines to pick up the ink confined in the grooves. The resultant print is actually a paper mold of the plate. The lines of the print stand in bold relief above the surface of the paper, as does ink on an engraved calling card. Engraving, aquatint, mezzotint, soft ground, drypoint, lift ground, and other approaches employed in intaglio work are all printed in exactly the same manner. Each of these approaches, however, offers a unique look to the final print. (See the illustrations in the section devoted to intaglio printing.)

The stencil process—serigraphy.

This is the newest print medium to be seen in exhibition circles. In the last twenty years or so in this country, we have seen serigraphy rise phenomenally. How is it accomplished? Various stencils, which when printed one over the other will make a completed print, are fixed upon separate screens of silk stretched tautly over wooden frames. Each separate frame is an individual printing unit. Paint is introduced at one end of the frame and *squeegeed* across to the oppo-

A COMPARISON OF GRAPHIC ARTS MEDIUMS

Process	Relief	Intaglio	Planographic	Stencil
Common Name	(a) Woodcut (b) Wood Engraving	Etching Engraving Aquatint Drypoint, etc.	Lithography	Serigraphy or Silk Screen
Materials	(a) Plank-grain Wood (b) End-grain Wood, Linoleum, etc.	Copper Zinc Plastics, etc.	Limestone Zinc Aluminum Plates, etc.	Silk Organdie Nylon, etc.
Basic Tools	Knife Gouge Burin, etc.	Etching Needles Burins Acids Grounds, etc.	Litho Crayon Tusche Litho Rubbing Ink, etc.	Squeegee Screen Nufilm Glue Tusche, etc.
Type of Press	(a) Household Table-spoon (b) Washington Press or Letter Press	Etching Press (Clotheswringer type)	Litho Press (Sliding, scraping pressure)	None
What Prints?	Prints what is left of the original surface	Prints what is *below* the surface of the plate	Prints what is drawn *on* the surface	Prints open areas of the stencil
Line	(a) Black line on white ground (b) White line on black ground	Etching—ends squared Engraving—swelling Drypoint—soft, fuzzy	Crayonlike (granular) As with a pen As with a brush	Brushlike Pen Crayon
Value	Black or white	Greys obtainable through linear treatment or through aquatint, mezzo, etc. Wide range possible.	Wide range of possibilities from delicate grey to rich black.	Color—unlimited
Texture	(a) Grain of the wood block (e.g., pine could be utilized in the print). (b) None	Textures are man-made or man-controlled.	Stone given a grain by lithographer prior to drawing. Unlimited variations in texture possible.	Silk leaves its texture on the print.

site side, forcing the pigment through the "open" silk areas onto a sheet of paper directly under the screen. *Those areas of the stencil left "open" are the areas to be printed—i.e., the image; those stopped out by the stencil are the negative or nonprinting areas.*

The diagram on the opposite page allows a whole view of some of the similarities and differences that obtain between the various print mediums.

SOME QUALITIES OF PRINTS

If we set aside, for the moment, the personal reasons, desires, or drives that lead individuals to make prints in one medium and not another, let us attempt to analyze certain other reasons for their particular choices. In other words, we may ask, "What specific qualities are inherent in each method of printmaking?" Or, "What are the advantages and disadvantages of each medium of printmaking?"

1. LITHOGRAPHY. Stroking a lithographic crayon on a prepared stone surface presents a line or tone that is grainy, dark, or light—dependent upon the pressure employed when drawing it. The line may be fine or coarse, subtle or powerful, wiry or heavy (see Figs. I-23, 24, 25, 26, 27, 28, 30, 32, 37, 40) . Forms may be modulated from light to dark and dark to light with ease. The stone surface responds to every "kiss" of the crayon. Drawing on stone seems to resemble drawing on paper except that it "feels" different. It appears, at times, that you work on a sort of permanent, 4-inch-thick piece of paper.

Using a brush filled with *tusche,* a liquid variation of the lithographic crayon, you can paint stark black lines and areas on the stone (Fig. I-31) , create toothbrush spatter effects (Figs. I-29, 31, 39) , produce experimental acid-textures (Figs. I-35, 40) , tints, washes, drybrush treatments, mixtures of crayon and tusche (Figs. I-31, 39) , and an infinite number of other solutions to meet your particular requirements. There are few, if any, physical obstructions barring the way of your visual ideas on stone.

The "look" of the lithograph, therefore, may be dry, crayonlike, crisp, coarse, grainy, or seemingly luscious. It can be "wet" as a watercolor painting, scratchy as a white-line drawing on a black ground, or mottled and corroded as an old stone wall (see Fig. I-38) .

For those who feel most "at home" with crayons, brushes, pens, and the materials and tools employed in drawing and painting, for those who do not feel averse to exercising when printing from their stones, for those who seek a medium that possesses the property of multiplying original images exactly as they are conceived, lithography provides an admirable vehicle for expression.

2. WOODCUTS AND WOOD ENGRAVING. Bold contrasts of black against white, powerful vigorous lines and forms, stark simplicity and startling complexity are the hallmarks of the woodcut (see Figs. II-1, 4, 7, 8, 10, 12, 13). If drawing a knife along a block of wood sets up a series of sympathetic vibrations within your nervous system, if directness of expression and ease of printing are a consideration, if you feel no need for greys or softly modulated forms in your work, then the medium of woodcut will amply satisfy your needs.

A wood engraving, on the other hand, may offer the eye a rich network of white lines on a black ground; this variant of the relief method of printing can be mathematically precise, picturesque and romantic, vibrant and energy-laden, simple or complex (see Figs. II-5, 6, 21). If the line made by a *burin* in an *end-grain* block of wood seems to fit in with your visual idea, if patience and strength of will keynote your personality, if you have something that needs to be said in the unique manner of this medium, then by all means seek out your tools and materials and start on your first wood engraving.

3. ETCHING AND ENGRAVING. Here you will find delicate linear effects similar to pen-drawn lines (Fig. III-4) posed against frenzied, powerful strokes (Fig. III-7), patterns and textures that range the spectrum of possibilities (Figs. III-1, 2, 6, 8, 9), dynamic black areas and wispy grey effects (Fig. III-14). Color, form, line, texture, and spatial solutions rival the easel painting; the face of the intaglio print is exciting and provocative.

If working on copper or zinc plates with acids, needles, and burins seems challenging, if your preparatory sketches "cry out" for the crisp line of engraving (Fig. III-11), for experimentation in textural effects possible with soft ground (Figs. III-12, 15, 16, 17), for the soft, velvety quality of the drypoint, the tonal potentialities of aquatint, mezzotint, or lift ground (Figs. III-10, 13, 14, 17, 19), if you relish the work and play involved in wiping and printing plates on a hand-powered etching press, then there is no doubt but that you will enjoy making intaglio prints.

4. SERIGRAPHY. Diversity seems to be the keynote of what is happening in serigraphy. These screened images range from the colorfully

simple to the "simply colorful"; they are as varied as the personalities of the artists who make them.

Silk screen printmaking may provide the vehicle through which you express color in precise forms and knifelike edges (Figs. IV-17, 21, 22), freely brushed images and "painterly" suggestions (Figs. IV-12, 19, 20). Color may be applied flat (Fig. IV-21) or mottled (Fig. IV-23), transparent (Fig. IV-20) or opaque (Fig. IV-21), heavily textured (Fig. IV-18) or thin (Fig. IV-16), with a minimum number of screens (Fig. IV-13) or the employment of many (Fig. IV-12).

If the actual "stuff" of color is a real requirement in your work in that you need the look and feel of real paint, if space and economic considerations are limiting factors, if you desire ease in printing truly large editions of your prints, here is a color medium to fit anyone's and everyone's mode of expression.

A note of warning.

There is implied throughout this book one salient point: Just as it would be puerile to equip a home woodworking shop with expensive power tools and other equipment when one had neither the need nor the inclination to make something useful of wood, so would it be questionable to acquire a mulitiplicity of techniques in printmaking when one had no visual ideas to express, no need to communicate anything of significance to anyone.

"I desire that soon it [lithography]
shall be spread over the whole world, bringing much good
to humanity through many excellent productions,
and that it may work toward man's greater culture . . ."
                                              SENEFELDER, 1817

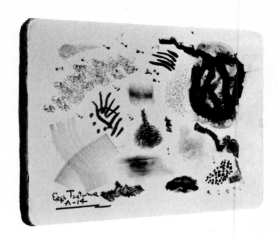

I

The Planographic Process:

Lithography

MOST OF THE LITERATURE on lithography, with but few exceptions, states that it is necessary for an artist to draw upon the stone, and for a professional printer to "pull" or print the edition. Why has this dualistic assertion persisted? Most of the writer-experts in the medium of lithography claim that it takes many years of painstaking apprenticeship, much trial and some error, and an enormous output of labor before one can successfully "pull" a fine edition of prints from stone. They believe that the pursuit of qualitative printing is too strenuous for the artist, too complex a procedure for him to learn, too wasteful of his invaluable time.

While all or part of these claims may be true, and it is not my intention to pursue the matter, it is almost categoric that the artist who does not print his own lithographs from the stone does not begin to know the potentialities of lithography. A lithograph printed by the artist who conceived it can be more than a mere drawing which was made on stone and then transferred to paper. In the very act of printing a lithograph, it is possible, and many times desirable, to alter, change, improve, or strengthen one's initial visual statement. Only to the artist who has explored the printing process is the medium of lithography meaningful and challenging.

No claims are made here that the artist, after scanning this chapter, will be able to surpass the professional artist's printer in the art of *printing* a lithograph. It is possible, however, for an intelligent person in the arts to become aware of the problems involved in the process of planographic printing, and to solve these problems in a comparatively short time, in accord with the needs of his own visual statements.

AN EXPLANATION

Perhaps I can best explain what lithography *is* by first stating what it *is not*. Lithography is not a process or medium within the field of graphic arts wherein one mechanically copies on a stone a drawing previously made on paper or other substance. It is not a descriptive term that applies to the purchase of the services of a professional artist's printer in lieu of proving one's own work. It is not a mysterious process that somehow spews up multiple originals called lithographs, as some Victorian-minded folk still would have us believe. It is not a precise, scientific, critical medium.

Yet, it involves the act of drawing; some artists *do* have their work attended to by professional printers; its chemistry, while not mysterious, has not yet been reduced to a sole explanation which finds unanimity; it is a scientific process—in a manner of speaking.

Briefly, lithography is the total act of imparting a visual idea upon a stone with a grease-containing substance, chemically treating it, verifying it, and printing it yourself in order to control and multiply the visual statement.

At this point there may be readers who, hypothetically, will exclaim, "But, all you have described is the process of lithography as it has been known and practiced since Senefelder first discovered it—over one hundred fifty years ago!"

There is an element of truth in this exclamation which makes it necessary for us to explore the situation more thoroughly.

There are altogether too few artists who have been aware of the "oneness" of lithography; too many artists have never realized their potential in this particular medium; too many artists have accepted the myth of the owner-printer of the press: that it takes an artist to draw upon the stone, and a printer to print it. Yet, allow any artist who has accepted this dualism to print his own work, and the thesis of the necessity for the professional printer vanishes.

To begin with, he is likely to note there is an obvious visual difference between his work when printed by himself and when printed by other hands. Moreover, he must face up to the following questions: Which of the two most closely resembles his own "handwriting"? Over which has he exercised greater control? What is the role of the printing process in the total creative act? Is it desirable to be free to alter, change, improve, or strengthen the image on the stone during its printing? Which is the most satisfying to the artist? What limitations are placed upon the artist who allows the printer to print his work? What limitations are evident when printing one's own work?

The author has seriously considered these problems for many years. He has observed scores of artists and art students in the past decade in his graphic arts workshop. Working with these alert people—discussing these questions, analyzing the problems—has resulted in a further confirmation of the point of view that in lithography, as in all the other graphic arts, the artist must act as his own printer.

On the assumption, then, that you have something of significance to say, and wish to learn how to integrate this visual idea within the technique of lithography, let us begin to clarify the problem step by step.

1. GRAINING THE STONE. You will have to "grain" or grind a new and clean surface on the stone which will carry your pictorial idea.

2. DRAWING OR CLARIFYING YOUR PICTORIAL IDEA. On this freshly grained stone, you will place your graphic image.

3. ETCHING THE STONE. The image will be treated chemically to allow you to multiply this original work many times.

4. PROVING THE STONE. After taking a few trial proofs, and making any corrections, additions, or alterations of the original idea, you will make an edition of lithographs—pulling as many prints as meet your needs.

Now, let us examine these steps in sufficient detail to guarantee you a successful experience in the making of a lithograph. The materials necessary for each step are included at the head of each section. Since the graining operation precedes all others, these are the tools and materials necessary for that operation:

Fig. I-1. A levigator.

A graining table (or a sturdy waist-high stool if you can work out-doors).

Two or more lithographic stones, and a levigator (Fig. I-1), or a small stone.

Carborundum, numbers 180 and 220.

A stone file or rasp.

Snake slips.

A water supply.

For a more detailed description of the materials and tools, consult the Appendix under "Lithography." Now, let us start our adventure with lithography.

MAKING A LITHOGRAPH

Lithographic stones, in order to receive your visual idea in some grease-contained substance, must be freshly grained. The last image contained on the stone surface must be ground off thoroughly. This grinding action may be accomplished with a levigator (see Fig. I-1) and an abrasive on a single stone, or by two stones with an abrasive between them. We will describe the latter method, since levigators are rare instruments.

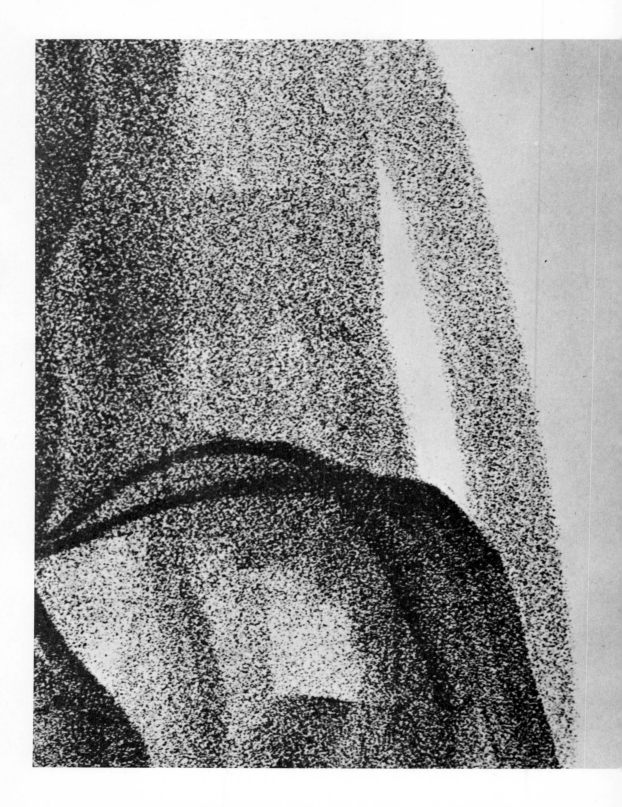

Fig. I-4. Applying carborundum to a wet lithographic stone.

Graining the Stone.

Sprinkle a liberal tablespoonful of #180 carborundum on a stone you have just wet with water (Fig. I-4). With your fingers, distribute the carborundum on the surface of the wet stone so that the abrasive covers well. Then, slide another wet stone of approximately the same size on top of the first one and begin to spin it counterclockwise (Fig. I-5). Do not allow the top stone to travel too far beyond the edges of the bottom stone or you will have an unevenly grained pair of working surfaces. To compensate for the concavity or convexity that will result if the stones are always ground in the same positions—that is, with the bottom stone always on the bottom, and the top stone always on the top—be sure to reverse the relationship at each grinding.

You will discover, after a few minutes of grinding, that the carborundum, and the muck that accompanies it between the stones, is becoming creamier and lighter in value. Also, that the stones are becoming more difficult to spin. What is happening is that the carborundum is beginning to cut into the limestone surface and is scoring it or roughing it up to impart the peculiar lithographic grain upon which you will work. Oddly enough, the stone which will look and feel as slick and glossy as polished marble is actually a surface composed of minute hills and valleys. This has been caused by the abrasive action of the carborundum. When you observe the muck getting stiffer and creamier, and before the top stone becomes too difficult to spin, gently slide

Fig. I-5. "Graining" the stones.

the top stone from the bottom one. Hose down both stones with water to remove completely all the particles of carborundum. Inspect your stones to make certain the "ghost" (the image that was previously drawn on the stone) is gone. If it still remains, it may be worth while to repeat the #180 grinding again. Some "ghosts" are difficult to remove. After hosing down the stones once more with water, sprinkle a liberal tablespoonful of #220 carborundum on the surface of the bottom stone. Spin the top stone in the usual graining manner for only about three minutes this time. This is suggested to keep from "flattening" the grain. Again, gently slide off the top stone, and hose them both thoroughly with water. Stand them on edge to allow the excess water to drain off. Then, place them on a flat surface.

With clean newsprint, blot off the excess water with as many sheets as are necessary. Inspect the stones when dry for any ugly scratches that may mar certain tonal areas (if you intend to work, or *do* work in such a manner as to require a perfectly flawless surface.) Otherwise, you need not be overly concerned at this point. Unless you intend to work out your visual idea immediately, it is useful to cover the newly grained stone with a sheet of newsprint paper. Tape it to the stone with decorator's tape or any other adhesive without having the tape cross your future working surface. If desirable, it is possible to grain the stones with an even finer surface. After employing #220 carborundum, use such grades of this abrasive as F or FF dependent upon the particular surface required.

Fig. I-6. Beveling the edges of the stone.

Cleaning the Edges of the Stone.

Prior to the final graining of the stone, it is suggested that you use a stone rasp or file to bevel the edges on all four sides of the stone (Fig. I-6) . Finish off the edges with pumice stone, Schumaker brick, or snake slip and water to keep these edges from picking up ink mechanically from the roller.

Various Approaches to Drawing upon the Stone.

Now that you have a freshly grained surface upon which to work, a visual idea in your mind or on a piece of paper, or a detailed compositional sketch, let us take a moment to reflect upon our problem. At this juncture, we have a man and a stone. It is assumed that the desire for communication through the medium of the stone will be of sufficient strength to overcome all considerations of strangeness of the material, fear of making "mistakes," or blind observance of rigid formulae for success.

It is not unusual for manuals of this sort to offer certain warnings to the beginning printmaker, who now sits and worries over his stone. He is usually told he must not, under any condition, touch the freshly grained surface with his fingers or hands. This, he is told, imparts grease to the stone and consequently ruins all of his work. He is further warned against speaking while working (fear of minute specks of saliva), sneezing, coughing, running his fingers through his hair, and many other "don'ts." Obviously, this effectively frustrates the beginning printmaker, or at best, causes him to work in an unnatural manner. I would like to minimize the printmaker's fear of these warnings without at the same time advocating their practice—unless, through experience with the medium and such unorthodox procedures, one maintains control at all times.

Leaving a margin all around the stone wide enough to support the travel of the scraper from start to finish across the stone (a margin of about one and one-half inches all around), begin to work out your visual statement with Korn's lithographic crayons, pencils, rubbing 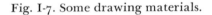 ink, tusche, or any combination of these tools (Fig. I-7). For those artists who work from a complete statement previously made on paper, and who therefore wish to transfer or trace that drawing from

Fig. I-7. Some drawing materials.

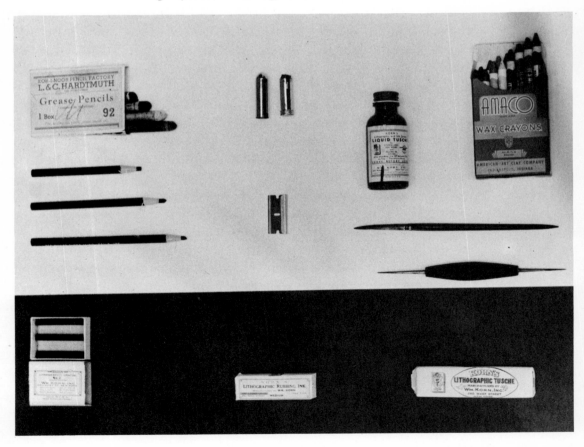

the paper to the surface of the stone, it is recommended that the back of the sketch be rubbed with conte powder or crayon (sanguine). When laid gently upon the stone, conte or red side down, and traced with a hard pencil, the bricklike color tracing will appear on the surface of the lithographic stone.

It is well to point out at this time that the image on the stone will print in reverse from that which you now see. If, after verifying the reversed image by means of a pocket mirror, you are satisfied with that image, all is well. However, if you have a complete drawing from which you want to work, and you do not want it reversed, remember to trace it backwards onto the stone. Having done this, you can look at your drawing in a mirror and know how to proceed.

For those who prefer a more direct beginning, just proceed to work out your visual ideas with your tools: *lithographic crayons* and *pencils* (these drawing instruments are not unfamiliar to artists or art students; employ these grease crayons and pencils in your normal manner), *rubbing ink* (rub the tip of your finger well over this specially prepared grease block and "paint," draw, or smudge with your finger on the stone), and *tusche* (this is similar to working with India ink and a brush; the grease is suspended in liquid form and can be used with brush or pen to obtain solid, rich black lines or areas; a variety of grey values can be obtained by mixing tusche with distilled water—as in wash drawing). One further bit of advice is offered those who seek to exploit the grain of the stone through sole use of the crayon: Keep a supply of well-sharpened crayons at hand, and work from the hardest to the softest varieties; that is, start with a number 4 crayon and work towards the number 1; from the lightest values to the darkest.

For those who are freer in approach, more experimental, or who have no qualms about using any material so long as it serves the visual end in mind, for those who would employ *scratching techniques* (using razor blades or sharp, steel needles to obtain white lines in black crayon or tusche areas), *rubbing* with cloths, fingers, chamois (rub these over your block of lithographic rubbing ink to charge them, then apply lightly to the stone), *scraping* (using a razor blade to scrape middle tones from black areas, or whites from middle tones), *jumping* a knife across the surface of the stone (a device which obtains a dotted white line on a black area), *burning* (using diluted nitric acid with a brush for certain textural effects), *brushing or spat-*

tering asphaltum thinned with turpentine onto the stone as a substitute for tusche, etc., I merely wish to point out that tools and materials may be as imaginative as your visual solutions. (Figure I-8 shows a stone covered with many experimental textures.) All you need bear in mind is that you must work with a substance containing grease (soap, lipstick, children's crayons, etc.) on a stone surface which can be clarified, altered, or improved with any device or tool you can fashion before, during, and/or after your visual statement is "etched." Further, it is well to keep in mind that you are not attempting to imitate on stone what can more easily be accomplished on a sheet of paper. There seems to be no "best" way in unfolding a visual statement on a stone surface.

Etching the Stone—*Theory and Some Practice.*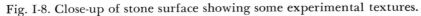

Assuming you are tentatively satisfied with your "drawing" on the stone, you will need to prepare it for printing. This step is known as "etching" the stone, though it is a very poor description of what oc-

Fig. I-8. Close-up of stone surface showing some experimental textures.

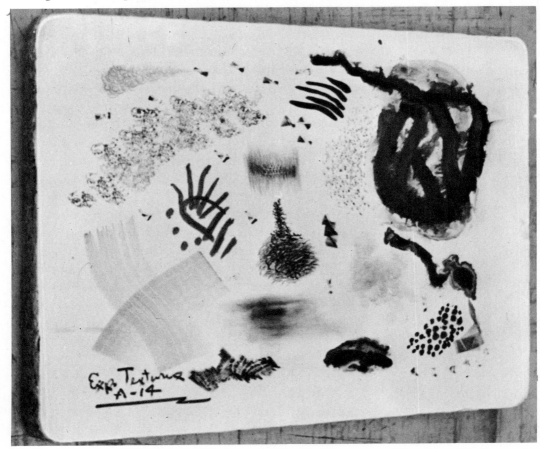

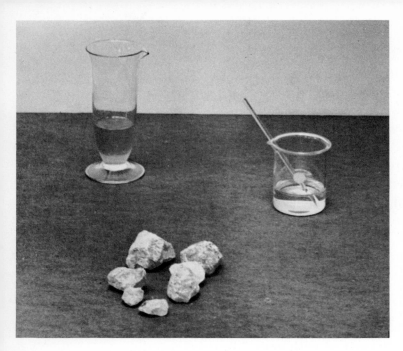

Fig. I-9. Gum arabic crystals plus water equals the base for the etching process.

curs. You have produced your work with a material that is soluble in water. (Rub a water-soaked rag over a litho crayon drawing on paper to prove this statement.) We will need to use water in the printing process. How do we meet this problem? A syrupy mixture of gum arabic crystals and water, upon contact with your "stone-drawing" will make that crayon or tusche work insoluble in water. With the addition of a somewhat critical amount of nitric acid, the "etch" further desensitizes the undrawn areas to the reception of ink, sensitizes further the drawn areas to the reception of ink, and when dried, locks around each grease spot or "mountain" to guarantee the repetition and multiplication through printing (all other things being equal) of all of the lines and values as they were initiated by the artist. This is how you will proceed:

Add enough water to two ounces of gum arabic crystals to make a syrupy mixture when the crystals dissolve (Fig. I-9). This is not a critical formula; you can add crystals or water to produce a mixture which, when tested for its viscous quality by dipping your closed thumb and index fingers in the mixture and pulling apart gently, will allow almost a quarter of an inch of tension before breaking. Strain 1½ ounces of this mixture through a discarded nylon stocking or wad of cheesecloth into a clean graduate or jar. The impurities seen in the mixture are merely bits of bark from the acacia trees that provide the gum.

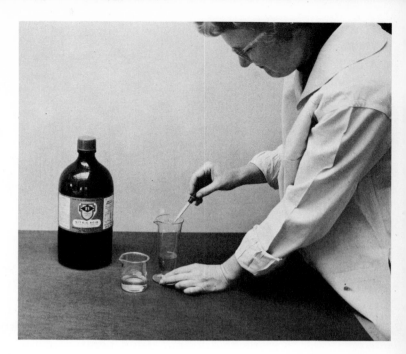

Fig. I-10. Adding nitric acid to the base of gum arabic.

You now add nitric acid to the gum (Fig. I-10). It must be remembered that temperature, humidity, the age and temperature of the nitric acid, the particular qualities of the stone on which you have worked—all of these, separately and in combination—are the variables with which you must contend. Our procedure is based not upon a static formula, nor on an intuitive approach to materials, but rather on an intelligent understanding of the role of the "etch." The more grease you have used in your work (the softer pencils, crayons, and tusche impart more grease to the surface than do the harder ones), the stronger must you "etch" the stone. Tusche, scratching with needles or other sharp points, scraping with knives or razor blades, tints of tusche, and all other special treatments of the stone, except pure crayon work, require a much stronger etch than normally is used. As many as 75 drops of nitric acid in 1½ ounces of gum arabic have been used successfully with experimentally worked stones at the Graphics Workshop of the University of Southern California.

A tentative test of the correctness of the "etch" for normal crayon work is obtained by using a base of 1½ ounces of gum arabic (we use 16″ by 20″ stones) and adding drops of nitric acid to the gum arabic mixture, which, when stirred and swabbed on the margin of the stone, will cause an effervescence in a very short time (about 20 seconds, though I wouldn't always hold a stopwatch on this aspect of the proceedings). The number of drops of acid added to the gum is al-

Fig. I-11. Etching the stone.

most certain to be different with each stone, and even with the same stone at different times because of the variables already mentioned. Do not let this disturb you; an average number of drops of nitric acid for an average crayon approach to a base of 1½ ounces of gum arabic is somewhere between 15 and 50 in Southern California, for this particular method.

Your own test trial on the margins of your stone will provide your particular solution for the conditions that exist at the time you are working. If you have employed any techniques other than that of drawing with the crayon, you must "etch" your work much more. That is, the "etch" should froth almost immediately upon contact with the test margins of your stone. When you are satisfied that your "etch" meets the requirements for your particular stone and the work upon it, you are ready to proceed with the process of "etching" your lithographic stone.

Etching the Stone—Practice.

Pour about half of the "etch" on one of the margins of your stone. Quickly, using the heel of your palm or a 3-inch rubberset brush, carry the "etch" over the entire stone surface (Fig. I-11). Add the remainder of the "etch" as required—in an area that has previously been covered with the gum and acid. Move the "etch" around on the stone for a few minutes—especially, move it from the light grey to the dark tonal areas and the scratched or scraped work. Now, with

Fig. I-12. Damping the paper.

newsprint, quickly blot the excess gum from the stone. Repeat this at least twice. Before the gum gets tacky, rub the etch down to a fine, thin coat with the palm of your hand, a rubber squeegee, or a pad of cheesecloth. Fan the gum dry or let it dry of its own accord. Most experts agree that the etch should remain on the stone at least overnight or longer. It is possible, however, to go ahead with the process when the gum is dry to the touch.

Damping the Printing Paper.

At this point, we should begin to prepare our paper for its role in the printing process. Fine prints are pulled on damped paper. In lithography, paper is damped to allow it to become soft enough to make good contact with the ink. Yet it should be hard enough so that it holds together without tearing when run through the press and "peeled" from the stone. The question then arises: What paper or papers meet these conditions or requirements? Obviously, a complete list of such papers would be overpowering. It is suggested, therefore, that beginners may obtain fair to excellent prints on Fiesta Cover Stock. Many professionals use Rives or Arches for their editions, and pull proofs on Basingwerk Parchment. For those who desire to experiment with different varieties and weights and qualities of paper, it will be found that each type has an optimum dampness. In employing a damp press, use a slightly wet sponge on both sides of the Fiesta Stock (Fig. I-12).

Stack the paper, in groups of seven to ten sheets, between wet blotters. Placing the cover on the damp press, weight it down with a large litho stone. Leave the paper in the press overnight to allow it to damp evenly. You may prefer to use a damp book made of oilcloth, rubber sheeting, or some of the new plastics. If so, cut a piece that is about two and one-half times the size of your blotters. Wrap the damped paper and the wet blotters in this "cover," then place a large drawing board on top, and a stone on top of the drawing board. There are both advantages and disadvantages to particular papers employed in lithography. It is suggested that you try a number of papers before selecting one for your personal use. Because the test of a good paper is closely related to your own manner of working on the stone, it is therefore difficult, if not impossible, to suggest a panacea for all the paper evils that may occur.

Ink and Roller Preparation—Theory and Practice.

Our next step in the printing procedure is concerned with the preparation of the ink and roller. First, let us examine the part played by the roller in the printing process. The lithographic hand roller is an instrument of primary importance in the production of an edition of fine prints. It must, then, be in excellent condition so that it may impart ink to the grease-drawn areas upon the stone. It also has certain other functions: It must be able to remove ink from the stone when rolled quickly across the surface, and should be able both to reduce the dampness of the stone surface and increase it when necessary. When the roller performs these functions satisfactorily, it can be said to be in good condition.

The lithographic hand roller is similar in appearance to the old-fashioned rolling pin. Averaging about 14 inches in length and 4 inches in diameter, it is made of a solid wood core, covered with a heavy flannel cloth which has an outer covering of horse or calf skin mounted rough side out. The seam on a good roller is barely visible, and can remain so if it is not scraped over by the spatula. The handles of the roller are fixed rigidly to the core. You use the roller with two leather hand grips or cuffs which protect the hands and at the same time allow the roller to turn easily when it passes over the ink slab or stone. These heavy leather grips or cuffs are easily made by the printmaker. They are cut from heavy scrap leather so as to produce two rectangles of 3½ by 4 inches.

How do you condition a new roller? It first should be smeared with a soft lithographic varnish until it can absorb no more. At this point it will begin to drip varnish. (Set the roller handles on two short lengths of 2″ by 4″ lumber and catch the varnish drippings on waste paper placed beneath the roller.) Scrape off the varnish with a spatula, first against the grain of the roller, then with the grain. You might engrave an arrow on one of the handles of the roller pointing in the direction of the grain. Here is a suggested method for scraping the roller: Place one end of the roller securely against the frame of the press. Moving your body towards the press, allow the other end of the roller to come to rest against the line of your belt. The roller should be supported at this point without the use of your hands. Grasp the spatula with both hands, as with a draw knife, and raise slightly the edge nearest yourself. Now, pull the spatula firmly across the length of the roller. Wipe the spatula clean, and proceed to scrape the rest of the varnish from the roller. You will observe that bits of nap from the roller come off during the scraping. Be careful not to scrape across the seam of the roller. Doing so will leave an ugly line when inking your stone.

Add a harder varnish, #6 or #7, to the roller and work it into the leather with your hands. Then, pass the roller over the ink slab firmly for about 15 to 20 minutes. This will pull off the excess nap. Scrape the roller down and repeat this procedure until there is a minimum of nap appearing on the ink slab. Clean the ink slab thoroughly after each rolling period. At this point, you can add a line or two of ink across the ink slab, and roll the roller in ink for several sessions of about 15 to 20 minutes each. Scrape the roller well each time before proceeding to the next session. Your roller should soon be in good condition. Keep it this way by rolling it in fresh ink and scraping it down even on days when you do not intend to print. If you have to leave it idle for a week or so, wrap the roller in wax paper, aluminum foil, or any substitute. On leaving it idle for a month or more, it is recommended you coat it with mutton tallow or Vaseline, or a convenient substitute. This protective material would have to be removed completely from the roller before your next printing session.

If you have acquired an old or secondhand lithographic roller, the procedure in reconditioning it is essentially the same as for a new one. You might, however, go over the roller with a wire suede brush and some white gasoline. This will tend to pick up the nap of the leather and at the same time will remove some of its hardness. From this point, proceed as with a new roller. Turpentine, according to old-line lithographers, should never be used on a leather roller. They say it will harden the leather and make the roller unfit for use in a very short time.

Black crayon ink, when purchased in one-pound cans, will be found to be of a convenient size for both workshop and classroom. It is quite stiff and must be scraped out of the can with a heavy ink knife or its equivalent. Temperature and humidity will affect lithographic ink, though this is difficult to believe when first you try to scrape some out of a can. It is recommended for each printing session that you take out from this ink can no more than a heaping tablespoon of ink. This must be worked up with the ink knife to a point where it will flatten slowly by the force of gravity when piled up in one corner of the ink slab. Here is one method for working up the ink: Employing a heavy ink knife, bear down with considerable force upon the gob of stiff ink and then pull the knife across the whole ink slab as many times as it takes to cover the whole slab with a thin film of ink. Scrape it all up together again and repeat this several times. You will find that this has altered somewhat the original consistency of the ink. If you are printing on a particularly cold morning, you may have to add a tiny amount of varnish to the ink to get it to the proper state. It will not take long to find, through experience, both the quantitative and qualitative essentials involved in ink preparation for lithography.

Another method for preparing your ink is to bear down on the gob of ink with the ink knife and rock and twist the knife from side to side as you let the knife travel towards you in a straight line. When you reach the end of the slab, or have over-ridden the ink, turn the ink knife over and scrape up all the ink. Turn the knife over again so that the ink is once more on the bottom side and repeat this as many times as is necessary to condition the ink by trying the gravity test mentioned above.

Removing the Etch and Regumming the Stone.

Remove the old "etch" by hosing it down with water. You can verify the removal of the "etch" from the stone surface by passing your fingers lightly over the margins of the stone. You will once again feel that peculiarly slick surface. Using just pure, strained gum arabic

Fig. I-13. Washing out the drawing.

(which you have mixed prior to washing out the old "etch") regum the stone and rub this down to a fine thin coat with a soft, clean woolen rag. Polish this coat of gum to a *very thin* layer. Let it dry of its own accord, or fan it dry.

"Washing-out" Procedure.

Pour a liberal amount of turpentine in the center of the stone and, with a clean woolen rag or a small sponge, carry it all over the stone and wash out the drawing (Fig. I-13). Do not be alarmed at the sight of the stone, which should be quite messy and appear as though you have "erased" all of your crayon and tusche drawing. The blackness of the turpentine mess is caused by the removal of the lampblack from the crayon or tusche by the solvent. Since lampblack is chemically inert and plays no part in the chemical process of printing— though, of course, it does allow the artist to see the relative values within his composition—we have no cause for worry. The grease-drawn areas which are important still remain in the same position in which they were drawn, modelled, or brushed on, and in the same degree of lightness or darkness in which they were conceived, even though, at the moment, they cannot be seen appreciably well. When you are certain you have washed out your composition, dry the turpentine by fanning the stone.

Inking the Stone—the "Roll-Up."

Sponge the stone thoroughly with clean water and carry it quickly to the press bed. Keep the stone damp at all times when the stone is "open," that is, when the grease-drawn areas are unprotected by a coat of ink. Pass the ink-charged roller over the ink slab several times to freshen it up a bit, damp the stone with a sponge, and quickly pass the roller up and back across the entire stone. You do not need to bear down heavily upon the roller handles. Remember to turn your knuckles all the way down each time you pass the roller up and back across the stone. This, you recall, is done to start the roller in a new place each time in order to distribute the ink more evenly across the image on the stone. You will observe the stone slowly accepting ink from the roller (Fig. I-14), especially as the moisture on the surface evaporates from the friction created. You may slow down the rolling speed, but don't slow it so much that you smut the stone and clog all of the open areas. Before the stone dries out—and you should be watching it carefully—redamp the stone with your sponge once more, and recharge the roller on the ink slab. Continue inking in this manner until the composition approximates your original visualization. At this point, you do not need to redamp the stone surface.

Proving or Printing Procedure.

We are now ready to "prove" our composition (Fig. I-15). Make certain, first, that the stone is placed in such a position on the bed of the press that the scraper will travel across the entire compositional area. Also, check to see that the scraper is smaller than the width of the stone and wider than the "drawing" on the stone. Now, take a sheet of newsprint and place it on the surface of the stone. (Holding your paper at opposite corners allows you to center a sheet of paper quite easily.) On top of the sheet of newsprint place two clean blotters, and on top of all place a sheet of tympan board or red fibre board (Fig. I-16). The tympan should be well greased with mutton tallow on its upper surface. This allows the stone to go through the press much easier than would otherwise be possible. Check to be certain that the leather scraper is also well greased, since the scraper and the tympan will be forced to "kiss" and slide against each other under great pressure. Rotate the screw on top of the yoke of the press in a counterclockwise position so that the scraper is drawn higher up under the yoke.

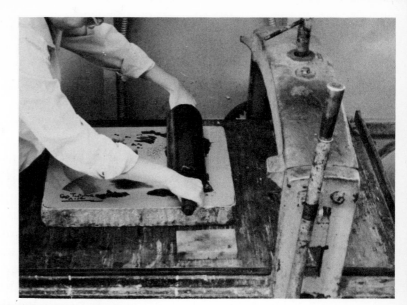

Fig. I-14. Rolling up the image.

Fig. I-15. Showing the inked stone on the press bed.

Fig. I-16. Printing paper, blotters, and tympan placed on stone.

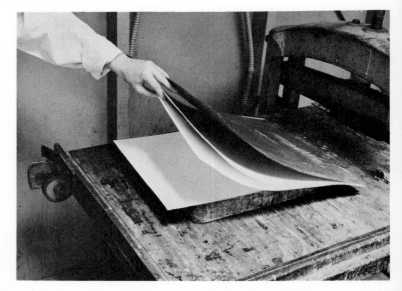

Now, push the press bed so that the leading margin of the stone comes under the scraper; or, stating this another way, until the scraper is resting over the leading edge of the stone, and between three-quarters to one inch or more *on* the stone. In order to approximate the correct pressure for the particular stone upon which you are working, pull down the press lever until it seems locked in position. Now, turn the screw which runs from the scraper box up through the yoke of the press clockwise all the way down to the stone until you can turn no more. Release the press lever and turn the screw approximately two turns more. This is merely a rough estimation of the correct press pressure. It will be necessary to adjust and readjust the pressure for optimum results. Perhaps it should be stated at this time that it is most important in the printing process in lithography to use a minimum of means in producing the maximum effect possible in the print, that is, a minimum of pressure, ink, varnish, etc. Now, pull down the press lever (Fig. I-17) and crank the stone through the press with an even motion (Fig. I-18). Stopping at any point before you reach the opposite margin from your starting point will cause a dark line to be made through the print parallel to the position of the scraper in the press. Do not go beyond the stone, that is, do not allow the scraper to run off the stone under its present press pressure, or you will crack or damage it. Allow the crank handle to come to rest, release the press lever, and, being sure to hold the tympan down firmly with your left hand, smartly pull the press bed back to its original position with your right hand. Remove the tympan and blotters, and then slowly peel the print from the stone as you follow the exposed stone with a damped sponge (Fig. I-19).

Be sure that the stone is damped all over before stopping to examine the proof. On examination, you may find that the proof is quite light and not yet up to full strength. Proceed to roll up again and prove the stone until the print is rich and equal to your design. At this time, you may substitute your damped printing paper for the newsprint. The difference between the dry proof and the damped print is always astonishing. Re-ink for each print as above, remembering it is better, and wiser, to under-ink at first. It is possible to pull fifty or more prints with this one etch, if you work quickly, but not nervously, and with a minimum of press pressure and ink enough to keep your blacks rich and your greys in scale.

Fig. I-17 (above). Pulling down the press lever.

Fig. I-18 (left). Cranking the stone through the press.

Fig. I-19 (below). "Pulling" the print.

Reworking the Design.

Assuming you want to rework your design, the following suggestions are offered:

1. IF YOU WANT TO REMOVE LINES OR TONAL AREAS: Ink the stone as though you were going to pull another print. Fan the stone dry. Press powdered resin into the inked design and, with a damped water sponge, wash off the excess resin. Work into the stone by scratching, scraping, grinding, or any other way of accomplishing your purpose with any device or instrument that will do the job. Do not get into the area of bas-relief, however; all that is necessary is to expose the surface of the stone. This may be done with razor blades, litho needles, sandpaper, steel wool, knives, etc. Sponge the stone clean once more with water. Spread a medium "etch" over the stone and, with a watercolor brush, paint in a stronger "etch" over the newly worked lines or areas. Thin the gum with newsprint. Dry. Proceed as though this were the first etch on your stone. Refer to page 17. (Damping the printing paper) and proceed from there.

2. IF YOU WANT TO ADD WORK AND REOPEN THE STONE: Ink the stone as though you were going to pull another print. With a small piece of sponge, wash over the whole surface of the stone with acetic acid glacial. Keep the acetic acid moving on the surface for a few minutes, and then wash it off with much water. Fan the stone dry. Add the new work, and re-etch as though just beginning. In many instances, if you wish to add a good deal of new work, it would be better to re-grain the stone.

3. FOR ADDING AND REMOVING WORK ON THE SAME STONE: Perform operations 1 and 2 in their respective localized areas. It is in situations like this where the artist, after having pulled an edition of prints, can learn for himself his potential in lithography. There are limitless numbers of approaches that can be utilized on stone. The medium of lithography, in spite of all that has been done with it and to it, has by no means been exhausted as a medium for visual communication.

WORKING IN COLOR LITHOGRAPHY

Let us assume, for the moment, you have gained some experience in the printing of your own lithographs in black and white to the degree that you know exactly what you want to do and how to do it, within certain limits. Remember, we are not expecting that an artist, with a little experience, can surpass the professional printer in the techniques of printing. Nor are we willing to give up to the professional printer that aspect of our complete conception—the actual pulling of our print. For we know by now what the potentialities of the medium are, especially during the printing process, and this phase of the total process we can leave to no one else.

Color lithography is rapidly making converts of many of our printmakers, who formerly worked only in black and white. It has opened new avenues for exhibition and distribution; there is a vast, untapped potential for the American artist. The limitations of lithography in color do not exist in the medium per se; the limitations, and there are undoubtedly many, exist because of the academic and apathetic attitudes of the defenders of the "I'll-draw-it, you-print-it" school. When artist-lithographers finally concede to themselves and each other that lithography in color is something they can and must do themselves, we may look to a creative and healthy outburst of prints to challenge the best work of the recent European upsurge in color lithography. And now, back to the workshop.

Preliminary Color Sketch.

This may be worked in transparent water color, colored crayon, pastel, tempera, oil, casein, duco, vinylite, or any other color medium on paper. However, none of them singly or in combination with each other will duplicate the color quality of the lithograph—nor should they be expected to equal the colored inks. There are some of us who prefer to work up a color lithograph, not from a sketch prepared in another medium, but directly from the colored imprint of the first stone. Others merely want to use the preliminary sketch as a base from which to explore. Still others work out a complete color statement from which they do not wish to deviate. Whatever your approach to this aspect of the problem, there are certain steps we all will take together.

Work up a full-scale color visualization of your idea in any color medium, using as many colors as you desire. (It takes a separate stone for each color, unless through combinations of the colors selected the number is reduced.) At this point, before you consider doing a

17-stone color lithograph, it would be well to keep our earlier principle in mind: Use a minimum of means for the maximum effect. Now, analyze your sketch in terms of its component parts. How few stones will be needed to equal and, in a sense, go beyond this color statement? Shall we revert to the orthodox yellow, red, and blue stones, in that order of printing, for our desired result? How many color possibilities are available through the use of two stones? Three stones? Four stones? The following diagrams show the theoretical possibilities (Fig. I-20).

Substitute any colors for the letters in any of the diagrams and, by knowing *what,* when mixed with *which,* produces WHAT, you can determine the basic possibilities in color. We can see, by Fig. I-20, that it is theoretically possible to arrive at fifteen different hues in many values and intensities from four stones, dependent upon what and how we "draw," the order of printing, the lightness or darkness of given areas in the stone, the textures, etc., etc. When we realize,

Fig. I-20. Color possibilities with two, three, and four stones.

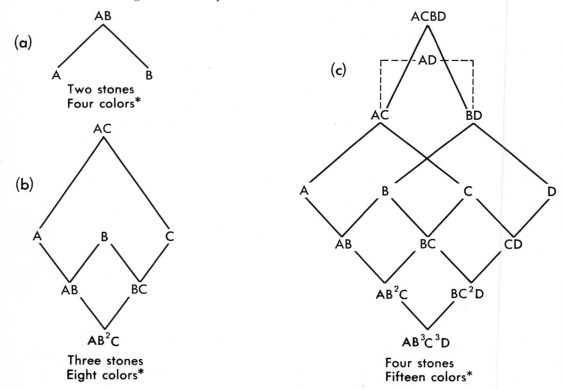

* Including the color of the paper employed in the print.

too, that our palette is similar to that of the painter, the potential is still further heightened. Color lithographic inks need not be used in their pure form "right from the can," but can be greyed, lowered in value, made more or less opaque, etc.

Your preliminary color sketch can be regarded as your master or key drawing. All you need do to make it such, is to draw two hairline crosses at diagonally opposite ends of the sketch, outside the design border by at least a full inch. Make certain, as well, that the crosses will still be within the printing area of your stone or stones. (It is entirely possible to do multicolored lithographs on a single stone by printing one color, graining off slightly, reworking the next color drawing, reprinting, regraining, and so on.)

Method 1. Working from a Master Color Sketch.

Assuming we are going to do a 3-stone lithograph, make a separate tracing from your master sketch of each of the three colors to be used. Be sure to employ a nonoily tracing paper. Powder the back of the tracing with conte powder and trace off color *A* on your stone, making certain you have also traced off the registration crosses accurately. Work up your design using crayon, tusche, or rubbing ink. The necessary step of translating your color sketch into values ranging from black to white will not seem difficult after you have completed your first color lithograph. After drawing the design, etch and proceed as before, with black and white. The only difference obtains from the fact that you will not use black ink with which to print, and you probably will be using a composition roller. Therefore, your most dense blacks drawn on the stone will only be as dark as the color you roll up on the ink slab. (It may be useful to mention that for color work we have found that a slab of plate glass 24 by 26 inches, with a clean piece of white paper underneath, is useful in "seeing" the colored ink.)

It is not necessary, after the etch and wash-out, to roll up the stone in black ink. If the etch has been "right," you may go ahead with your first color. Remember to check that your registration marks are printing clearly on your prints. Pull a few proofs, and then use your good printing paper. (It is also possible to pull color work on dry paper.) On completion of a quantity of prints slightly larger than your intended edition, allow them to dry flat under pressure. When dry, use a new, single-edge razor blade and cut out the shaded triangles at opposite ends of each sheet of paper, as in (a) , Fig. I-21, or, using a paper punch, cut circles at the intersection of the crosses, as in (b), Fig. I-21.

Now, you may use the same stone again (if it is all you have) and grain it down with #180 and #220 carborundum, but not sufficiently to remove the ghost. When dry, trace color *B* on the stone, work it up, etch, and roll it up in color *B*. (If you are fortunate enough to own many stones, and have gummed down stone *A* after having rolled it with ink so as to preserve the work, proceed to trace color sketch *B* on the second stone, and draw, etch, wash out, and roll up with color *B*.)

Being careful to check top and bottom of your print, place the top triangular hole directly over the shaded triangle on stone *B*; then, sighting (as though down a rifle barrel) through the bottom triangular hole, place it over the bottom shaded triangle on stone *B*. Run this through the press, and on removing you will see the effects of two colored inks on your print. Go ahead and pull all the prints that have previously been printed with color *A*. Proceed with color *C* in exactly the same manner. When through, you can study the total effect of the print and through self and group analysis of the work, plan your next, and your next, and your next lithograph in color.

Fig. I-21. Registration devices.

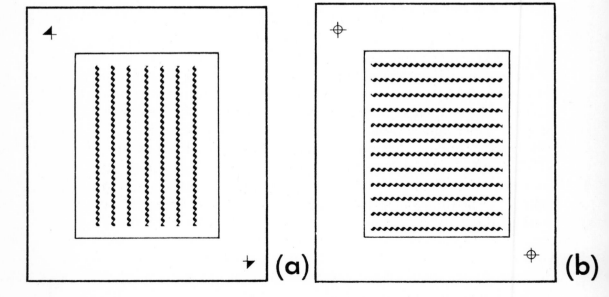

(a)   (b)

Method 2. Improvising A Color Lithograph.

With no master sketch to work from, but merely with a definite picture rectangle traced on the freshly grained stone, begin to work up a design. Place two registration crosses at diagonally opposite ends of this picture rectangle and work up your idea with tusche and/or crayon. Redraw the registration marks with tusche and a fine pen point. Etch as with a black and white print. Lay out a palette of litho ink near your ink slab and mix a tentative color on the slab. Roll the composition roller in this ink on the slab. Wash out the stone and roll up with the particular color you have just mixed. Take a few trial proofs and examine the print. If you approve the partial effect, go ahead and run a number of them. If not, run just a few, and alter the ink color by adding a sufficient quantity of another ink to produce a quite different effect. Run a few, or as many as you like. Repeat this, if you desire, to obtain a number of small editions of stone #1 in a number of different colors.

Take any one of the proofs and, with water color or any other color medium, add work in another color or colors to clarify your visual intention. Use another freshly grained stone or the same one (see Method 1) to work up color #2. You may trace off color #2 from this color sketch and then reverse it before tracing onto the stone. Or, you may merely look at your proposed intention on the sketch, and remember to work backwards on the stone. (You recall that all direct-method printing surfaces reverse the image.) It may be helpful to arrange a mirror and your sketch so that you can glance in the mirror to see your color sketch in its proper relationship to the act of drawing on the stone (see Fig. I-22).

Fig. I-22. Device for reverse drawing.

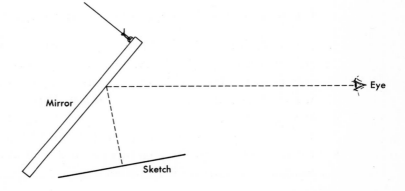

Draw, etch, wash out, roll up, and print stone #2, using the same procedures recommended in Method 1. Be careful in laying your prints on the inked-up surface of stone #2. Follow the registration procedure in Method 1. Continue this for as many stones as are necessary to complete your color statement.

Method 3. Color Lithography by Subtraction.

This is another 1-stone, multicolored method which involves much careful planning beforehand. It concerns working up the complete image in crayon and/or tusche on the stone, then placing registration marks arbitrarily at opposite ends of the picture rectangle, etching, and then sitting down to work out the following: It is theoretically possible to print the entire stone in any one color, then to subtract portions of the stone and print what is left in another color, then to remove still more from the stone and print the remainder in a third color, and so on. The drawing, etching, wash-out, roll-up, and printing and cutting of the registration triangles is done as has been suggested in other parts of the book.

Removal of certain areas in this method may be accomplished by scratching, graining out with a small glass bottle stopper and carborundum, painting out with a strong solution of nitric acid and a small amount of water, etc. Remember to etch the recently removed portions of the stone. Also, in stopping between successive color printings, it is advisable to roll up in black ink with your leather roller and gum down with about 6 drops of acid to 1½ ounces of gum arabic. When you wish to start again, wash off the old etch, gum down with a very thin layer of gum; then dry, wash out with turps, sponge stone with water, and roll up with your new color.

NEW APPROACHES TO LITHOGRAPHY

At this juncture, it should be apparent that attempts to circumscribe lithography are destined to fail. The techniques and experiments to be described here are only suggested as possibilities for research. It is only through the widest dispersion of such information that printmakers will evolve and exchange techniques in the solution of craft problems. Certain lithographs seen in recent print exhibits have furnished cogent evidence that the range of approaches within this medium is limitless.

Experiments with Acid on Solid Tusche. (See Fig. I-35.)

Cover a freshly grained stone with two coats of tusche, leaving an adequate margin on all sides of the stone. Work out a design with conte crayon on the dried tusche, or trace a drawing on its surface. Using an almost undiluted nitric acid solution and a brush, begin to paint out the lightest areas. The acid will soon begin to bubble on the limestone surface; the longer it is allowed to remain, the lighter will that area become. Further, a peculiar textural effect obtains if this is done slowly, by degrees. Keep a water-wet sponge in one hand to stop the acid action, by wiping whenever desired. Move on to the succeeding dark tones until the image emerges from the blackness. Pour unacidulated gum on the surface when you have finished the design. Dry and thin the gum. Set the stone aside for a day or so, and print in the usual manner.

Experiments with Lithotint. (See lower third of Fig. I-36.)

Wet a freshly grained stone with water. Work into it with a solution made of a stick of solid tusche and warm distilled water. Complete your design. Mix a very strong solution of gum arabic and nitric acid, enough to make the etch "boil" on contact with the stone. Thin and dry the etch, and print in the usual manner.

Experiments with Acid on Heavy Crayon. (See Fig. I-39.)

Heavily applied crayon drawings, effects obtained with lipsticks, or bars of soap may all be etched and printed as in the manner of lithotint. They all need *very strong* etches.

Experiments with Transfer. (See Fig I-28.)

There are many other possibilities for transfer in addition to the traditional method of making a design with crayon and/or tusche on paper, then damping the sheet, laying it face down on a freshly grained stone, and pulling it through the press several times to get it to offset onto the stone. By direct or indirect methods we can transfer the imprint of net, chiffon, or other loosely woven fabrics. We can offset fresh proofs from any other graphic arts medium. We can even revive an old technique of Senefelder's and transfer all or part of the printed matter from books. Remembering that this is a chemical method of printing, our only concern is to transfer a grease image onto our stone. Obviously, we can transfer relief images, if they have a grease coating, or flat surface images having a similar property. In other words, we can transfer from the "thing" itself, or from a proof (called a "counterproof) of the "thing." The transfer should be treated with gum and a trace of nitric acid, thinned and dried, and then printed in one of the traditional manners.

Variations and New Directions.

When we consider printing with color rather than with black ink, and using more than one technique in the same lithograph, it becomes apparent that we cannot but hint at the potential of this field. Here then, are a number of isolated possibilities:

1. RUBBED TONES: (See upper right section of Fig. I-24). Using a stick of lithographic rubbing ink, rub your finger over it to load it with the grease and then pass it lightly over the area to be covered. The harder you press on the stone, the darker will the particular effect print. To avoid ugly marks or fingerprints, load the ink-smeared finger after each light pass over the stone area. It is also possible to use a piece of silk wrapped around the particular finger employed. Do not under-etch rubbed tones, or you will have to rework them later on in the process.

2. GUM ARABIC AS A "STOP-OUT": (Some possibilities may be seen in Fig. I-31). A solution of gum arabic and water may be employed with a brush to "stop out" (keep white) certain areas of a proposed print. The inbetween areas can accept crayon, tusche, or even an inked roller across the surface without interfering with the whites under the gum. A toothbrush may also be employed to spatter gum on the surface of the stone, if a series of white dots is required. Gum arabic may further be utilized to paint out the borders of a stone on which you intend working. This is used by some printmakers to keep the margins clean.

3. PEN AND INK, OR BRUSH AND INK: (See Fig. I-34). Grain your stones for this technique with FF or FFF carborundum. Use pen or brush or a pointed stick with tusche to make your composition. Dry-brush effects, if strongly etched, will print exactly as they look on the stone.

4. THREE-VALUE LITHOGRAPHS OR MANIÈRE-NOIRE: There are two popular ways of working a lithograph so that it emerges as a white-grey-black print. (a) Brush two coats of tusche in your design area. With a razor blade, scrape the black down to a grey. Using various needles and points, pick and scratch out the whites. Add the blacks with crayon and/or tusche. Etch this type of stone very strongly. Print in the usual manner. (b) Paint out the whites with a solution of gum arabic. Take a heavily charged lithographic ink roller, after the gum has dried, and roll it from several directions over and back across your composition. Allow the ink to "sit" for a while before proceeding. Using tusche, paint in your blacks. Etch and print as usual.

5. ASSORTED MATERIALS: A piece of string or cord could be dipped in tusche and pressed onto a stone, or the string could first be printed on a sheet of paper and then offset onto the stone. (The black line in the lower right section of Fig. I-31 suggests this possibility.) Various textiles could be inked and offset onto the stone (as we can see in the background of Fig. I-33). A small brayer covered with tusche or asphaltum could be applied to the stone surface. (See the sky area of Fig. I-36.) Fine sandpaper or emery paper may be used to soften certain edges. A broken or otherwise useless knife may be employed to "jump" (leave a linear pattern of particular white marks) on the stone surface. A piece of sheet gelatin placed on the crayon drawing on the stone may be used in this fashion: In areas (dark greys or blacks) where you desire white lines without scratching them in, trace through the gelatin with a hard pencil. Removal of the gelatin will reveal a particular kind of white line on a dark ground. Steel wool can also be employed for special effects, particularly in dark or black areas. A little imagination and a great need can add an infinite number of other tools and materials to this series of suggestions.

Experiments in Intaglio Methods.

Coat a stone with at least two layers of tusche. (Do this in your picture rectangle, of course). With a lithographer's needle or an etching needle, scratch your composition through the tusche layers so that the stone is definitely exposed. Apply a very strong etch to this type of print. This yields a white line technique on a black ground.

For the opposite effect, do the following: Within the picture rectangle, brush in two coats of gum arabic. Allow the gum to dry. Trace your composition lightly on the gum surface. Now, with a lithographic needle or its equivalent, engrave your design. Be sure to cut through the gum. When the image is finally completed, rub some thin ink in the lines. Remove the gum, roll up, etch, and print. In this instance, you will have a black line technique on a white ground.

Using Zinc and Aluminum Plates.

Senefelder called his original discovery of lithography "Chemical Printing," which accurately describes the total process. Accordingly, zinc and aluminum plates are receptive to lithography as are many other substances, such as glass, iron, rubber, etc. The advantages of using zinc over stone include the obvious weight factor, being able to purchase them already grained, and a negligible cost factor per plate. The disadvantages to the artist in using zinc and aluminum are found in a more limited freedom in working. Obviously, if we were to subscribe to the printing of lithographs by others than the printmaker himself, there arises the not undesirable notion of mass-produced works of fine art which can be turned out on a lithographic offset press. Further, if these works of art are to be conceived in color, with the printmaker drawing directly on each of his plates so that the camera does not interfere with his autographic quality, the result would encompass autolithographs in color. These now unknown prints would excel by far the present work of the machine. But, let us return to the use of these metal plates by the artist.

The lithographic process is exactly the same for metal plates as for stone with these few exceptions: (1) The plates must be counteretched before being drawn upon. (2) Different etches are employed for metal plates. (3) Many of the "experimental" scratching techniques are not advisable in metal plate lithography. Here, then, are the necessary procedures.

Place the plate in a hard rubber or enamelled photographer's tray. Mix a saturated solution of powdered alum and water to which you may add the slightest trace of nitric acid. With a clean, soft brush, move the solution over the plate for no more than 2 minutes. Remove the plate. Flood it with water, and dry it immediately (to prevent oxidation) . This is called the counteretch, which prepares the plate for your design. The plate is now quite sensitive. Follow the same procedures as for lithography on stone, bearing in mind that not all of the techniques apply (these things you will find out for yourself with the completion of your first metal plate lithograph). Though the etching procedure is the same, you must use instead of nitric acid the following etch: 3 ounces of gum, 1½ ounces of a saturated solution of bichromate of potassium, and ⅛ ounce of phosphoric acid.

Experiments Printing Water and Oil Colors Simultaneously.

Senefelder suggests that after a stone has been inked in an oil-base, colored ink, one or more water colors can be added to the design and printed off in one operation. Add two parts of gum arabic and one part of sugar to your color. Allow the color to remain on the stone a minute or so before you make the impression. What would be the result if we reversed the whole theory of lithography, and used oil instead of water on the stone to damp it, while we printed with a water-base ink?

Many times, through visual analysis, it is possible to glean much information that otherwise rarely, if ever, comes to light. Let us, then see what we learn from the study of the following lithographs in Gallery One.

A GALLERY OF LITHOGRAPHS—THE PAST

Three years before his death, at the venerable age of seventy-nine, Francisco de Goya y Lucientes tried his hand at the still new medium of lithography. Despite his physical infirmities—and they were many—his necessity for creation was resolved in crayon on stone. Among the lithographs Goya produced at this time was "Bravo Toro" (Fig. I-23), one of a series of four prints on bullfighting.

The autographic quality of the lithographic medium is revealed in a study of this particular print; the use of both crayon and needle are readily discernible in the grays, blacks, and whites of the image. The "handwriting" of a master is there for all to see. Goya's telling use of the medium places the viewer right in the arena with the brave bull; the entire thrust of the composition from upper left to lower right is offset by the powerful force of the bull.

Fig. I-23. Francisco de Goya y Lucientes: "Bravo Toro"

In contrast, the romantic, picturesque landscape by Eugène Isabey presents another approach to lithography—less heated than the Goya, more virtuosolike in technique. The content, as filtered through the sensibilities of an Isabey, required this particular manner. "L'Eglise Saint Jean, Thiers, Auvergne" (Fig. I-24) is a fine example of romantic nineteenth-century lithography. It is one of many lithographs commissioned by Baron Taylor for his 24-volume series of "Voyages Pittoresques et Romantique dans l'Ancienne France." The subtleties of dark and light, the textural variety, and pleasing effects combine to make today's viewer "like" such a composition quite readily. From a technical point of view, note the rubbing ink employed in the sky and middle-ground, the sparing use of the lithographic needle to scratch white lines or accent a roof, figure, or façade. Tusche is employed for black accents, while the main body of the composition is worked with crayon.

Fig. I-24. Eugène Isabey: "Eglise Saint Jean, Thiers, Auvergne"

It is not often that a man such as Daumier stalks on to the world's stage; but, when he does, the impact of his visual record remains as a challenge to all those who come afterwards. In "Rue Transnonain" (Fig. I-25) we get a glimpse of the topical lithograph that transcends the particular to become universal.

Seen against the background of history, this print emerges to protest the brutal, inhumane, senseless attitude of the military. France in 1834 was seething with restlessness, intrigue, counterintrigue. The silk weavers of Lyons went out on strike, followed by a general strike; in Paris, troops patrolled the streets to discourage the Parisians, and especially the Society of the Rights of Man, from setting up a sympathetic strike. It was said later that a shot was fired upon the passing troops from #12 Rue Transnonain. In retaliation, every man, woman, and child was killed who lived in that building. Daumier's print came out on the streets of Paris a few days later.

In more than four thousand lithographs and two thousand woodcuts, paintings, drawings and sculptures, Daumier recorded the face of his times decisively and incisively, with a social awareness that was sharpened on the stone of life.

Fig. I-25. Honoré Daumier: "Rue Transnonain"

Fig. I-26. Honoré Daumier: "Conseil de Guerre"

A crayon, a needle, a stone, and a fiery imagination; a compassion rooted in a love for his people, even visible in his satire; a swift worker, a politically mature man; this was the essence of Daumier.

In his later years, his line became even more incisive, and he was quick to utilize the technical advances in lithographic reproduction. His "Conseil de Guerre" (Fig. I-26) speaks eloquently for itself.

Fig. I-27. Gavarni: "Embuscade"

Of particular interest to the student is the lithograph, "Embuscade" by Gavarni (Fig. I-27). Since the artist is more usually known through his graceful delineation of the upper middle class female, her escorts, episodes, and attitudes, this print is notable as an exception to the rule. Granted, it has none of the power and dignity of a Daumier, but in the swiftness of the crayon on the stone, in the deliberately scratched sky area, the artist has gone beyond his usual formula. The suspense in the total image is overwhelming.

Another nineteenth-century artist worthy of our consideration is Odilon Redon, whose "Yeux Clos" (Fig. I-28) offers still another point of departure. In this case, the source of the lithograph lies deep within the dream, the inner life, the introspective individual. The mystic qualities of this head attract and tantalize the viewer. The textural aspect of the print suggests a "transfer drawing" (see page 33) which was reworked with crayon.

Fig. I-28. Odilon Redon: "Yeux Clos"

The world of nineteenth-century Paris comes to life in the lithographs of Toulouse Lautrec (Fig. I-29) —intimate scenes at the cafes, the can-can girls, the middle class on the grand boulevards showing off the latest fashions, the riotous color of the race tracks, the glitter and glamor of the theatre, and the vices, small and large, of ordinary mortals. Here in the color lithograph, "L'Estampe Originale," it seems that we are literally inside the studio of the lithographer, watching him at work. The print is pure Lautrec, both stylewise and technically—the lithographic rollers, standing on end in a slotted brace under the table in the lower center; the bowl of damping water and damping cloths on the shelf attached to the press at the middle left; the stone with paper and tympan over it being turned through the press by the printer in his skullcap and apron; the interested connoisseur critically examining the fresh proof while dressed in the height of fashion; the lettering, reminiscent of Japanese prints—as indeed the whole print reflects this obvious debt. All of this tends to speak of the artist and his life. Both by omission and commission in his work, no man can but reveal himself.

From a technical point of view, there are certain interesting features worth pointing out. Two registration crosses appear at the left and right center margins as do an inverted "L" and a straight line on the left and right top margins respectively. (See the section on color lithography for a detailed explanation of registration in color printing.) A tusche-filled brush was used for the linear aspects of the design and a toothbrush was employed to spatter the background. The color areas are laid in with flat tusche; there are only a few evidences of dry-brush technique.

No one could look for long at a work by Kaethe Kollwitz without sensing the deep, humanitarian love felt by this woman. The stark simplicity and resultant power of her pure crayon lithograph, "Stadtisches Obdach" (Fig. I-30), grows out of her sympathy, understanding, and alliance with the poor, the oppressed, and the miserable. The harsh social realism of Kollwitz is a bitter and brutal truth designed to stir the conscience of society. This is not a pretty picture; it should be evident that the artist intended it just as you see it. But throughout the work of Kollwitz—in lithography, etching, and the allied arts—there is ever present the dignity of man.

Fig. I-29. Toulouse Lautrec: "L'Estampe Originale"

Fig. I-30. Kaethe Kollwitz: "Stadtisches Obdach"

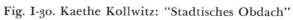

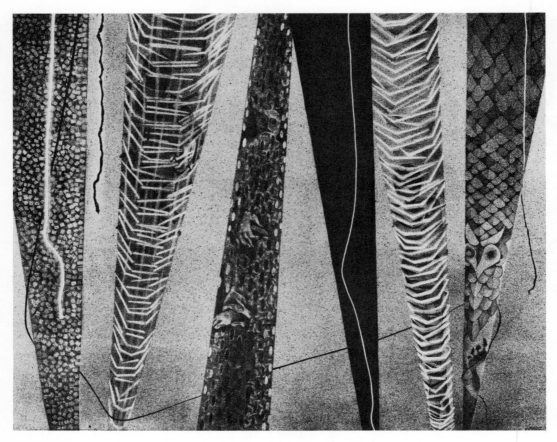

Fig. I-31. June Wayne: "The Witnesses"
Fig. I-32. Stow Wengenroth: "Meeting House"

A GALLERY OF LITHOGRAPHS—THE PRESENT

There are probably as many approaches to lithography today as there are people who practice it. No matter what one's particular preference, he will encounter many examples in black and white or in color that mirror his tastes. Recent innovations in the construction of a lithographic press hold even greater promise for the future.

"The Witnesses" by June Wayne (Fig. I-31) and "Meeting House" by Stow Wengenroth (Fig. I-32) offer a startling series of similarities and differences. Both prints are meticulous in execution; both artists have used or still use professional printers to make their editions. Where Wayne relies upon toothbrush spatter and scraped white lines for special effects, Wengenroth solely employs the crayon in the traditional manner, building up his image from light to dark. Where Wayne mirrors an inner world steeped in the symbolism of the unconscious, Wengenroth reflects the outer world. Both conjure up associations that travel far beyond the images employed, whether intended or not. These two prints are worthy of further study by the reader in terms of other similarities and differences pointed up by an instructor, or through discussion in a print workshop.

A combination of crayon line, tusche line, crayon area, and the imprint of a textile on stone suggested "New York, New York!" (Fig. I-33) to Sue Fuller. This imaginative use of materials, growing out of the content of the print, holds interesting implications for other printmakers.

Fig. I-33. Sue Fuller: "New York, New York!"

The portrait of "George Santayana 1952" (Fig. I-34) by George Biddle is a sensitive, searching, and penetrating visual analysis, accomplished in a most personal style. Fine pen strokes of tusche, evidence of needle scraping, smudging and stumping of the crayon, are unified in a clear presentation.

An otherworldly strangeness emerges from "Lament" (Fig. I-35) by Harold Paris. This is due not only to the specifics of the figures in the composition, but also to the technique employed. The visually interesting, yet peculiar textures result from the employment of acid on tusche-laden areas.

"Remnants" (Fig. I-36) a color lithograph by John Muench, offers a host of interesting treatments to the stone. Small composition rollers were used in achieving the sky area; the fish textures were made by dropping tusche in "puddles" of water on the stone; crayon, spatter, fine brush, and other devices may be noted on closer observation.

Eleanor Coen brings the world of the child to light in a most amusing and delightful fashion. Her color lithograph, "Bird in the Window" (Fig. I-37), clearly demonstrates her approach to this medium. Each stone, though incomplete in itself, adds another brick, as it were, to the building. The total effect is always one of a unity of many parts.

The moody, romantic "Nocturnal Cathedral" by Eugene Berman (Fig. I-38) provides a curious combination of rigid, scraped white lines and a crumbling, age-old Italianesque structure achieved with scraping, crayon, and washes of tusche. To further enhance the illusion of mystery, the print was pulled on blue paper.

The folklore of America received new vigor when William Gropper undertook to do a series of prints on his rich, thematic material. "Paul Bunyan" (Fig. I-39) is typically Gropper in its warm, humanistic, bold treatment. Crayon, toothbrush spatter, and tusche are employed in a direct, forceful manner.

"Farmer" (Fig. I-40), a study by the author, is a combination of crayon, tusche, and acid effects based on sketches made on a trip to Mexico.

No presentation of contemporary lithographs would be complete without a print by Max Kahn. "The Blue Cat" (Fig. I-41) portrays his sprightly style in one color over another until the image is clear. Kahn's sly humor pervades much of his graphic work.

Fig. I-34 (left). George Biddle: "George Santayana 1952"

Fig. I-35 (below). Harold Paris: "Lament"

Fig. I-36 (left). John Muench: "Remnants"

Fig. I-37 (below). Eleanor Coen: "Bird in the Window"

Fig. I-38. Eugene Berman: "Nocturnal Cathedral"

Fig. I-39. William Gropper: "Paul Bunyan"

Fig. I-40 (left). Jules Heller: "Farmer"

Fig. I-41 (below). Max Kahn: "Blue Cat"

WORKSHOP SOLUTIONS TO LITHOGRAPHIC PROBLEMS

During the Roll-up the Image Does Not Take Ink, or Does Not Get Dark.

Problem: Ink too stiff.
Solution: Add a drop or so of varnish, rework the ink and try again.

Problem: Insufficient ink on the roller.
Solution: Add a line of ink across the ink slab. Work up the roller. It should have a dull, velvetlike gloss evenly distributed over its surface.

Problem: Too much damping water on the stone.
Solution: Use less water in the sponge and use a small piece of another clean, damped sponge to "polish" the surface of the stone after damping with the first one.

Problem: The stone has been over-etched.
Solution: There is no remedy for this but to start anew.

Problem: There seems to be a film covering the stone.
Solution: Rub the stone with a rag and some fine pumice or carborundum while the stone is damped. Rub in some ink or asphaltum. Redamp stone. Roll up. Etch moderately. Print.

Image on the Stone Looks Well, but Prints Are Very Light.

Problem: Press pressure too light.
Solution: Assuming all other factors are controlled, turn down screw on yoke of press·one-half revolution, and repeat until print comes up.

Problem: Paper too wet.
Solution: Place between dry blotters, or wave in the air before use.

Problem: Paper too dry.
Solution: Place in damp press or sponge down individually before use.

Stone and Prints Go Darker with Each Succeeding Print.

Problem: Too much ink on roller.

Solution: Scrape down roller with spatula and remove some ink from the ink slab. Check results on next print.

Problem: Ink too thin.

Solution: Scrape off old ink from roller and slab. Use fresh ink with little or no varnish this time.

Problem: Stone under-etched.

Solution: Wash out with turpentine. Roll up as desired. With a small piece of sponge, wash over the stone with this solution: 10 drops of phosphoric acid, 10 drops of gum arabic in solution, and 1 ounce of water. After a few minutes wash off with clean water. Pass roller over stone once or twice and proceed to print. Should clear up after a few proofs. Repeat, if necessary.

Problem: Pressure too great.

Solution: Back off the screw on the yoke of the press and check results.

Stone Blacks Up Entirely.

Problem: You allowed the stone to dry while you were rolling. The roller deposited ink mechanically all over the stone.

Solution: Immediately flood the stone with water. Quickly charge your roller on the ink slab. With much pressure, high-speed rolling, and a kind of snap, briskly pass the roller over the stone to pick off the ink. The roller must be in excellent condition to accomplish this.

Paper Sticks to Stone when Peeling Off Print.

Problem: Paper too wet and soft.

Solution: Remove bits of paper from the stone with sponge and water. Place paper between dry blotters.

Problem: Ink too stiff.

Solution: Remove old ink from scraper and ink slab. Add varnish, rework. Or, add a drop or two of mineral oil in your damping water.

Borders of Stone Scum Up.

Problem: Mechanical adhesion, or unnoticed grease spots, or insufficient etch, or foreign matter.

Solution: With pumice stone, Schumaker brick, or snake slip, clean off borders on wet stone. Re-etch the borders with a strong solution of nitric acid and gum. (Use a brush to paint this strong etch on the stone.) Dry without having the etch get on the visual image. Wash off and print.

Scratches or Scraped Areas Fill In and Go Dark.

Problem: They have been under-etched, or over-inked.

Solution: Rework those areas and treat as in problem where stone is under-etched.

Streaks Across Stone Parallel to Axis of Roller when Rolling.

Problem: Seam of roller has been badly scraped.

Solution: It may be possible to eliminate this difficulty by rolling across the stone in another direction. Or, use a different roller.

Streak Across the Stone and Print Parallel to Axis of Scraper.

Problem: Stopping on the design when cranking the scraper across the stone.

Solution: If possible, pick off with the roller on the next inking.

Light Area in an Otherwise Well-inked Print. Stone Looks Good.

Problem: Check stone with a steel straightedge to determine if it is level. The light area may coincide with a hollow in the stone caused by faulty graining over a period of time.

Solution: Add another blotter or two under the tympan and check your results. If this hasn't helped, you have a choice of making a printer's makeready, or abandoning this stone until you level it by grinding.

Problem: Faulty coverage with the roller.
Solution: Roll the stone from several positions so that the design takes ink from different points of departure.

The Gummed Stone, on Drying, Forms a Myriad of Cracks.

Problem: Gum layer too thick, uneven, or effect of extreme temperature changes.
Solution: Add a tiny amount of sugar to the gum before putting it on stone.

Tones Inconsistent on Successive Prints.

Problem: Roller not charged evenly with ink.
Solution: Roll longer on the ink slab, turning the roller constantly.

Problem: Paper not evenly damped.
Solution: Place paper between dry blotters and save for another time. Prepare a fresh batch of paper taking care to avoid this difficulty again.

BIBLIOGRAPHY: THE LITHOGRAPH

Books.

Arnold Grant, *Creative Lithography and How To Do It*. New York: Harper and Brothers, 1941. 207 pp.

Audsley, George Ashdown, *The Art of Chromolithography*. London: S. Low, Marston, Searle, and Rivington, 1883. 24 pp.

Berri, D. G., *The Art of Lithography*. London: The Author, 1872. 46 pp.

Bregeaut, R. L., *Manuel Théorique et Pratique du Dessinateur et de L'Imprimeur Lithographe*. Paris: L'Auteur, 1827. 144 pp.

Brown, Bolton, *Lithography for Artists*. Chicago, Illinois: The University of Chicago Press, 1929. 102 pp.

Browne, Warren C., *Practical Text Book of Lithography; A Modern Treatise on the Art of Printing from Stone*. New York: National Lithographer, 1912. 231 pp.

Cumming, David, *Handbook of Lithography*. London: Adam and Charles Black, Ltd., 1919. 244 pp.

Dehn, Adolf Arthur and Barrett, Lawrence, *How to Draw and Print Lithographs*. New York: American Artists Group, 1950. 119 pp.

Griffits, Thomas E., *The Technique of Colour Printing by Lithography*. London: Faber and Faber Ltd., 1948. 110 pp.

Hartrick, Archibald S., *Lithography as a Fine Art*. London: Oxford University Press, 1932. 83 pp.

Hullmandel, Charles, *The Art of Drawing on Stone*. London: The Author, 1824. 92 pp.

Kistler, Lynton R., *How to Make a Lithograph*. A Visual Aid. Los Angeles: The Author, 1950. 25 plates.

Pennell, Elizabeth Robins, *Lithography and Lithographers*. New York: The Macmillan Company, 1915. 319 pp.

Rhodes, Henry John, *The Art of Lithography*. London: Scott, Greenwood and Son, 1924. 328 pp.

Richmond, W. D., *The Grammar of Lithography*. London: Wyman and Sons, 1886. 254 pp.

Senefelder, Alois, *The Invention of Lithography*. Translation from the original German by J. W. Muller. New York: The Fuchs and Lang Manufacturing Company, 1911. 229 pp.

Seymour, Alfred, *Practical Lithography*. London: Scott, 1903. 104 pp.

Waterlow and Sons, *Every Man His Own Printer; or, Lithography Made Easy*. London: Waterlow and Sons, 1859. 50 pp.

Wengenroth, Stow, *Making A Lithograph*. New York: The Studio Publications, Inc., 1936. 79 pp.

Periodical Articles.

Bjorling, Frank, "Proving," *National Lithographer*, pp. 28–29, Oct. 1914.

Bjorling, Frank, "Proving," *National Lithographer*, pp. 27–29, Nov., 1914.

Fisher, T., "The Process of Polyautographic Printing," *Gentleman's*

Magazine, 78: 193–196, Part I, 1808.

Ganso, Emil, "Technique of Lithograph Printing," *Parnassus*, 12: 16–21, Nov., 1940.

Goulding, Frederick, "Lithographs and Their Printing" (An interview with Mr. Frederick Goulding),

Studio, 6: 86–101, 1895.

Miller, George C., "Craft of Lithography," *American Artist*, 7: 21–23, Sept., 1943.

Seddon, R., "Producing a Colour Lithograph," *Artist*, 27: 22–24, March, 1944.

Related Information on Lithography.

"A. B.," "Lithography and Lithographer," *Burlington Magazine*, 30: 115–117, 1917.

Barker, Albert W., "Lithographic Notes," *Prints*, Vol. 7, No. 3, 139–142, Feb. 1937.

Bock, Elfriend, *Geschichte der Graphischen Kunst von ihren Anfangen bis zur Gregenwart*. Berlin: Propylaen-verlag, 1930. 716 pp.

Braquemond, Felix, *Etude sur la Gravure sur Bois et la Lithographie*. Paris: H. Beraldi, 1897. 94 pp.

Brown, Bolton, *Lithography*. New York: F. Carrington, 1923. 27 pp.

Copley, John, "Some Thoughts on Lithography," *Artwork*, 1: 247–252, 1925.

Craven, Thomas, *A Treasury of American Prints*. New York: Simon and Schuster, 1939. 302 pp.

Drepperd, Carl W., *Early American Prints*. New York: The Century Company, 1930. 220 pp.

Fielding, Theodore Henry A., *On the Theory of Painting*. (Appendix contains a manual on lithography.) London: The Author, 1846. 236 pp.

Glaser, Curt, *Die Graphik der Neuzeit vom Anfang des XIX Jahrhunderts bis zur Gegenwart*. Berlin: B. Cassirer, 1923. 585 pp.

Griffits, T. E., "The Herkomer Lithographic Technique and Applications," *The Penrose Annual*, XLV: 77–78. 1951.

Gutman, Walter, "American Lithography," *Creative Art*, 5: 800–804, 1929.

Heller, J., *Praktisches Handbuch fur Kupferstichsammler; oder, Lexicon der Vorzuglichsten und Beliebsten Kupfersticher, Formschneider, und Lythographen*. Hamberg: C. F. Kunz, 1823. 232 pp.

Holme, Geoffrey, editor, *Modern Woodcuts and Lithographs by British and French Artists*. With commentary by Malcolm C. Salaman. New York: The Studio Limited, 1919. 204 pp.

Jackson, F. E., "Lithography," *The Imprint*, 1: 18, 125, 171, 319, 1913.

Kistler, Aline, "Western Lithographers," *Prints*, pp. 16–25, May, 1935.

La Dell, Edwin, "Autolithography at the Royal College of Art," *The Penrose Annual*, XLVI: 46–48, 1952.

Lemercier, Alfred, *La Lithographie Francaise de 1796 à 1896 et les Arts qui s'y Rattachent*. Paris: Ch. Lorilleux and Cie., c. 1896. 358 pp.

McCaùsland, Elizabeth, "Lithographs to the Fore," *Prints*, 7: 16–30, Oct., 1936.

McIntyre, R., "Contrast in Lithographs," *Architectural Review,* 69: 135, April, 1931.

Okkonen, Onni and Puokka Jaako, *Suomen Taidegrafiikka.* Helsinki: Soderstrom, 1946. 160 pp.

Pennell, Joseph, *The Graphic Arts; Modern Men and Methods.* Chicago, Illinois: The University of Chicago Press, 1921. 315 pp.

Pennell, Joseph, "The Truth about Lithography," *Studio,* 16: 38–44, 1899.

Peters, Fred J., *Railroad, Indian, and Pioneer Prints by N. Currier and Currier and Ives.* New York: Antique Bulletin Publishing Company, 1930. 106 pp.

Peters, Fred J., *Sporting Prints by N. Currier and Currier and Ives.* New York: Antique Bulletin Publishing Company, 1930. 205 pp.

Peters, Harry T., *America On Stone.* New York: Doubleday, Doran, & Co., Inc., 1931. 415 pp.

Peters, Harry T., *California On Stone.* New York: Doubleday, Doran, & Co., Inc., 1935. 227 pp.

Peters, Harry T., *Currier and Ives, Printmakers to the American People.* New York: Doubleday, Doran, & Co., Inc., 1942. 41 pp. 192 plates.

Picasso, Pablo, *Lithographs 1945–1948.* Introduction by Bernhard Geiser. New York: C. Valentin, 1948. 66 plates, 14 pp.

Rothenstein, Will, "Some Remarks on Artistic Lithography," *Studio,* 3: 16–20, 1894.

Toussaint, Manuel, *La Litografia en Mexico en el siglo XIX.* Mexico: Estudios Neolitho, 1934. 68 plates.

Way, Thomas R., *Mr. Whistler's Lithographs.* Compiled by Way. Second Edition, London: G. Bell and Sons, 1905. 67 pp.

Wehrlin, Robert, "Reflections on Original Lithography," *Graphis,* Vol. 4, No. 22: 168–171, 192–193, 1948.

Weitenkampf, Frank, "A Revival in Lithography," *Independent,* Aug. 8 and 15, 1895.

Weitenkampf, Frank, "Art of Lithography in Portraiture," *Parnassus,* 2: 31–33, Feb., 1930.

Weitenkampf, Frank, *Famous Prints.* New York: Charles Scribner's Sons, 1926. 70 plates.

Weitenkampf, Frank, "Lithography for the Artist," *Scribner's Magazine,* 60: 643–646, 1916.

Weitenkampf, Frank, "Lithography for the Artist," *American Magazine of Art,* 9: 352–355, July, 1918.

Weitenkampf, Frank, "Painter-Lithography in the United States," *Scribner's Magazine,* 33: 537–550, 1903.

Weitenkampf, Frank, "The Making of a Lithograph," *New York Public Library Bulletin,* pp. 291–293, May, 1918.

Weitenkampf, Frank, "The War and Lithography," *International Studio,* pp. 61–62, Sept., 1918.

Whitaker, Charles H., "Lithography," *Architect,* 6: 241–244, 1912.

Zabel, Morton Dauwen, "Ink on Wood and Stone," *Art and Archeology,* 30: 66–68, 85, 1930.

Zigrosser, Carl, *The Artist in America.* New York: A. A. Knopf, 1942. 207 pp.

Zigrosser, Carl, *The Book of Fine Prints.* New York: Crown Publishers, 1948. 499 pp.

"Do not that which your finite members are capable of,
but that which, in moments of greatest tension,
you dimly guess at as a transient possibility
and let your fingers look to it how they can manage to get along."

MEIER–GRAEFE

II

The Relief Process: Woodcuts and Wood Engravings

THE ART of the woodcut has, for many centuries, been near to the pulse of the people. It has reflected the ideals, aspirations, significant dreams, the very heart of the common man. In "The Kiss of Judas" (Fig. II-1), a fifteenth-century woodcut, we obtain a glimpse of the direct quality of expression, the forcefulness and understanding of the anonymous printmaker of another day. This is not merely a remarkable wedding of form and content, or a beautifully unified example of picture with text; the associational overtones conjure up the life of five hundred years ago to express the "spirit of the times." There have been occasions in the past when the woodcut has sunk to the "lower depths" only to be revived again, at another time, as a multiple-original medium for visual communication. It has been sophisticated or simple, powerful or mannered, dynamic or obscure, idea-provoking or formalistic; it has been many things to many people.

For example, the people of Mexico are intimately acquainted with the art of the woodcut because it is the traditional medium of the *corrido*. The corrido represents a most significant aspect of the folk art of Mexico; it is a gaily colored, tissuelike piece of paper which weds a topical political, social, or economic satire, a pungent piece of poetry, or a trenchant ballad to a forceful woodcut—and is sold and sung in the market place and at fairs by a man with a guitar. For a few pennies one can acquire a corrido with an original woodcut designed by one of the leaders in the field of graphic arts in Mexico.

The folk art of the corrido reached its zenith with the work of Jose Guadalupe Posada. In his "The Jarabe Dance Beyond the Tomb" (Fig. II-2) we find some unusual techniques in addition to the start-ling content. Posada developed the metal relief print after many years of painstaking cutting on wood blocks. With this new technique, he drew on a zinc plate with an acid-resistant substance and allowed the mordant to do the cutting for him. The plate was then printed as a woodcut (see p. 81) . The skeletons, or *calaveras*, are favorite themes of the Mexican graphic artist; they grow out of the November cele-brations of the Day of the Dead, but are enmeshed with the very complex fabric of Mexican life. Through words and graphic images the page of "Calaveras" (Fig. II-3) speaks eloquently for itself. The illustrations were engraved upon ordinary battleship linoleum with single and multiple-toothed tools.

Corridos and calaveras engraved by Mexico's finest artists indicate the role played by the Mexican printmaker in his society. The corrido serves a need of the people of Mexico, and the printmaker serves his people. This was the way of the woodcut for many years.

In Japan the color woodcut played a similar popular role. Coinci-dent with the flowering of the people's theater (Kabuki) , the "Ukiyo-ye" color woodcut of that country was also widely supported. ("Ukiyo-ye" was a school of art which arose early in the seventeenth century, based upon the content of the transient or "floating world" of every-

Fig. II-1. Fifteenth-century woodcut: "The Kiss of Judas"

Fig. II-2. Jose Guadalupe Posada: "The Jarabe Dance Beyond the Tomb"

day life.) These were prints of famous actors and actresses in particular costumes and poses reminiscent of their "hit" shows, beautiful courtesans whose symmetry and elegance were tastefully recorded—as was their famous Yoshiwara district—and sensitive landscapes of Mt. Fujiyama and the surrounding countryside. All of this and more was seen in every household, or hawked on the streets, or pasted on the walls of buildings. Many of the first Japanese prints to reach Europe and thereby influence the course of Western art were initially used as wrappings for objects exported from Japan!

The color woodcuts of Hokusai (Fig. II-4) had a profound influence upon the work of many European artists, even as their works influenced his output. This "View of Fuji from Seven-Ri Beach" contains a number of educative principles relating to the Japanese woodcut: The "bird's-eye view" of the landscape was common to Eastern art long before the advent of flight; the asymmetrical compositions and sensitively arranged areas have always been the hallmark of the fine Japanese print; the transformation of the landscape

Fig. II-3. Taller de Grafica Popular: "Calaveras"

into a daring yet delicate new vision is also to be noted; the subtle gradations of color in the sky, water, and the beach suggest rather than represent the subject (in a print such as this, one senses the search for an "inner" truth or reality, rather than outward-appearing "facts"); the calligraphic quality of the letters in the upper left corner and their particular placement are essential elements in a very carefully balanced whole. (The calligraphic signs and symbols seen in Japanese prints, when translated, range from devices and signatures of the artists, artisans, and professional printers to descriptions of the scenes depicted, exact geographic locations, and words of sage advice.)

It may be of interest to mention that the rise of the "Ukiyo-ye" woodcut introduced a variant into the field through the creation of a division of labor within the total process. The problems of mass-production exacted new methods to meet the needs of the artisan class for these popular prints. The prints were made in the following way: (1) The artist's primary function was the design of the block. (2) The block was then given to professional block cutters. (3) After all of the blocks were cut, they were then handed over to professional printers who made the edition, and many times a fourth person acted as publisher. The visual unity obtained from this "split system" is still amazing to behold.

On the other hand, the creative printmaker of contemporary Japan takes great pride in his sole control over the destiny of his prints; he is designer, cutter, and printer—all of these—in himself. Once more the whole man does the whole work.

A GALLERY OF WOODCUTS

The selection of woodcuts, wood engravings, and linoleum cuts that follows is based in part on the normal distribution of these mediums seen in most exhibitions today. Color relief prints far exceed the number of black and white works.

"The Alchemists 2" (Fig. II-5) by Arthur Deshaies, when compared with "Homenaje al Heróico" (Fig. II-6) by Leopoldo Méndez, presents us with a pair of opposites from which we may glean much information. Both of these prints are wood engravings. Both of them were accomplished with the same kinds of burins. Both were done on end-grain wood. The only difference in the physical basis of the works is that the Deshaies print was composed of two blocks (the

Fig. II-4. Hokusai: "View of Fuji from Seven-Ri Beach"

join runs vertically down the middle of the print), whereas the Méndez print is made up of one block. Without belaboring the point, or pushing it beyond its limits, the obvious difference between these two prints lies in the conception and basis for motivation of each artist.

Antonio Frasconi, formerly of Uruguay, has recently come to occupy a notable place in American graphic arts. His color woodcuts have grown both in size and in stature since his arrival in this country. "The Storm Is Coming" (Fig. II-7) is an example of Frasconi at his best. Coupled with technical virtuosity is a rich, meaningful content. Frasconi has taken the popular art of the woodcut and clothed it in visually exciting color.

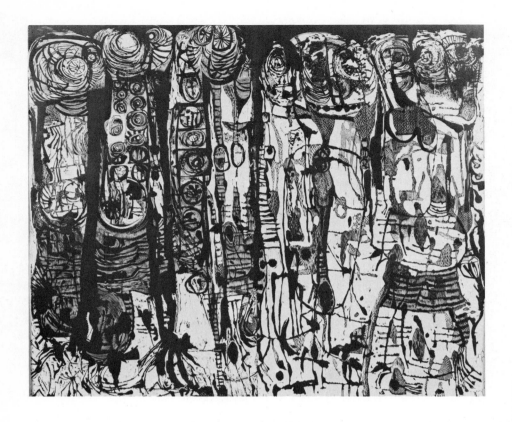

Fig. II-5 (above). Arthur Deshaies: "The Alchemists 2"

Fig. II-6 (right). Leopoldo Méndez: "Homenaje al Heróico"

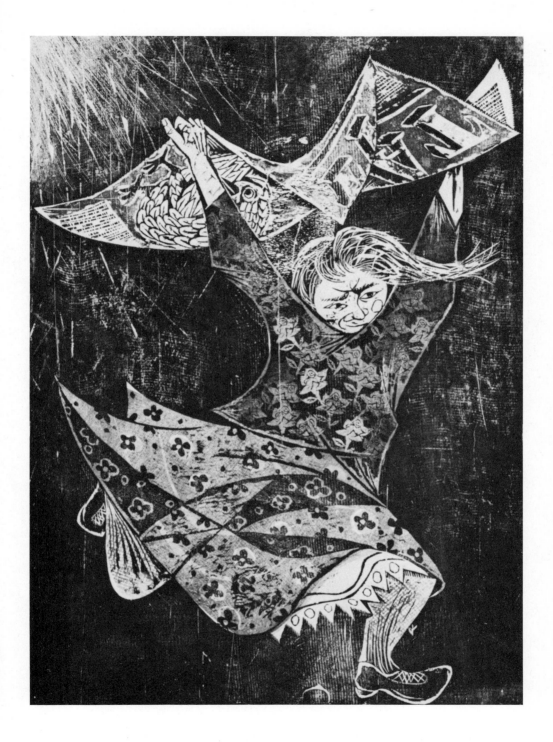

Fig. II-7. Antonio Frasconi: "The Storm Is Coming"

"Yo-yo Player" (Fig. II-8) by Seong Moy presents another approach to the woodcut. The carefully worked-out color separations that make up the individual color blocks show evidence of much thought and planning. Moy's wedding of the Eastern calligraphic line with Western forms is a very exciting visual phenomenon. Occasionally, as in this work, the directness of cutting into wood is lacking. It is almost a translation of a brush drawing.

Roland Ginzel's color linoleum cut, "The Significance of Integration" (Fig. II-9), may be taken to represent a new departure for this medium. This nonobjective work employs ordinary battleship linoleum as the medium through which the printmaker speaks. Using two separate blocks, one for the more linear black, the other for the yellow ochre forms, Ginzel challenges as it were with similar efforts in contemporary, nonobjective easel painting.

The woodcuts of Leona Pierce have a charm and vitality that grow out of her love and keen observation of children at play. She doesn't merely represent the world of the child, but transposes and transfigures the joy of living in a manner clearly defined. In "Leap Frog" (Fig. II-10) this feeling is expressed in bold, graphic terms.

Louis Schanker's color woodcut, "Birds in Flight" (Fig. II-11), points up the inner vision of a printmaker. Personal invention, the search for new ways of expression, the dynamics of design integrated with a visual idea—these seem to be apparent in the work of Schanker.

The strong graphic image of "Mother and Child" (Fig. II-12) by Sidney Chafetz stands boldly in the tradition of Expressionism. The emotional impact of the print grows out of a sensitivity to the medium and the content. Every stroke of the gouge and knife is clearly apparent in the final print; the play of black against white and white against black provides a rich, graphic experience for the viewer.

Another, and more recent, color woodcut by Antonio Frasconi, "Oil and Tilled Land" (Fig. II-13), presents forcefully a use of materials that is honest, decorative, and meaningful. Frasconi seems to delight in using the unworked wood grain (see the sky area) as an integral part of his composition.

Before we begin to cut into our own blocks of wood, it may be useful to explain our problem.

Fig. II-8 (left). Seong Moy: "Yo-yo Player"

Fig. II-9 (below). Roland Ginzel: "The Significance of Integration"

Fig. II-10. Leona Pierce: "Leap Frog"

Fig. II-11. Louis Schanker: "Birds in Flight"

Fig. II-12 (left). Sidney Chafetz: "Mother and Child"

Fig. II-13 (below). Antonio Frasconi: "Oil and Tilled Land"

An Explanation.

The relief method of printing is simple, direct, and comparatively inexpensive. That which remains on a smooth-surfaced block, after it has been worked upon by the printmaker, is inked and impressed upon paper.

To this day, there are writers on the art of the relief print who still make sharp distinction between the woodcut and the wood engraving. The *woodcut,* according to these experts, is worked on a *plank-grained* board, is cut with a *knife,* is essentially composed of *black figures on a white ground* and, with the possible exception of the Japanese approach to the medium, is utilized for dynamic contrast between black and white areas and lines. The *wood engraving,* on the other hand, is accomplished on an *end-grain* block of wood, is cut with fine *burins, gravers,* and other fine hand tools, is essentially an art form composed of *white lines on a black ground* and, with certain exceptions, is a more subtle combination of the black and white components of the print.

Let us summarize this traditional or "puristic" approach to the differences between woodcuts and wood engravings and compare it with contemporary practice:

Traditional Approach to Relief Prints.

	Woodcut	*Wood Engraving*
Material:	Plank-grained wood	End-grain block
Tools:	Knife, gouges	Burins, gravers
Effect:	Black figures on a white ground	White lines on a black ground

Contemporary Approach to Relief Prints.

The same distinctions prevail even today as regards materials and tools used in the separate mediums. True enough, contemporary society has added a vast number of new materials (masonite and other wallboards, various metals, cardboards, plastics, textiles, and other surfaces which will yield prints—these are used separately or in combination) and new tools (the flexible shaft—a power tool similar to

Fig. II-14. Misch Kohn: "Warrior Jaga-tai"

a dentist's drill, woodworking tools, and many unorthodox personal contributions) . It is in the final effect of the print, however, that there lies the vast difference between our approach today as compared with that of yesterday: In "Warrior Jagatai" (Fig. II-14) , a wood engraving by Misch Kohn, the artist employs the same materials and tools that were used in the past, but adds his own personal vision and craft to produce a new and exciting dimension to the medium. He breaks with tradition in that his wood engraving is *not* composed solely of white lines on a black ground. He has combined the power of woodcut with the subtlety and delicacy of wood engraving.

Artists such as Frasconi (Figs. II-7, II-13) , Moy (Fig. II-8) , and Schanker (Fig. II-11) , to name but a few, have added not only color and scale to the contemporary woodcut, but a whole new experimental attitude towards materials and tools, papers, and inks to fulfill their specific requirements for their prints.

There seems no reason, therefore, to plague ourselves with rigid limits arbitrarily imposed upon the relief print. There are too many exceptions to rules and principles taken by the practicing printmaker when faced with his visual problem. Let us encourage our relief print artists to continue in this way, solving their visual problems according to their own artistic vision.

Throughout the book, with no text to interfere with the image, examples of fine prints and enlarged details therefrom precede each new graphic arts medium to be studied. Each of the details is repeated in all of the chapters, allowing the reader an opportunity for comparative, visual analysis of the mediums both in technique and form.

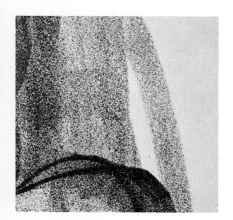

MAKING A WOODCUT

The tools and requirements for making a woodcut are simple and "homely" enough to allow their being worked entirely on a kitchen table. (This does not mean that the author is relegating this particular graphic arts medium to the culinary clinic, though there are certain obvious advantages to such an idea.) There is a certain direct quality in the woodcut, which is sometimes cited by unreceptive people as evidence of crudity, deficiency in technique, or a poverty of means of expression. The potential of the woodcut is only equal to the potential of the artist.

Materials and Tools for Cutting the Block.

Our basic needs are a block of wood, a sharp knife, some gouges, and an India oil stone, or its equivalent.

1. THE WOOD BLOCK. While cigar boxes and the ends of orange crates have been employed advantageously, there are certain woods which are held in high regard by the printmaker. For broad effects, pine is recommended, as are poplar, beech, bass, cherry, apple, pear, and sycamore—all cut parallel to the grain. Actually, any plank of wood that meets your needs, and is not so soft that it crumbles, will be useful. Plank grain is ordinary lumber commonly sold throughout the nation. If you intend to print the block by employing a press, it is advisable to secure wood that is type-high (about ⅞ inch). Some printmakers have recently taken to using wallboards (masonite, plywood, etc.).

2. THE KNIFE. The traditional knife of the woodcutter is of Japanese origin. It is made of a 4 to 5-inch blade held firmly in a slotted wooden handle by a tapered ferrule. It must be kept in fine cutting condition to function properly. Any knife, however, which "feels" well in your hand may be substituted for the traditional one. Buckland-Wright* mentions surgeon's scalpels, ordinary pocket knives and refashioned watch springs as excellent substitutes. The traditional knife, or its substitute, is usually held in the hand so that it may make a diagonal cut (about 45 degrees) into the wood, away from the edge of the line. Turning the block upside down, an-

---

* John Buckland-Wright, *Etching and Engraving* (London: The Studio Publications, 1953), p. 199.

other cut at the same angle will remove a "V-shaped" sliver of wood from the plank. If you prefer, instead of turning the block around, move your cutting fist through an arc of 90 degrees from its original position. Making an incision at this point will also remove a "V-shaped" sliver. All cutting should be done so that the base of each line is wider than the top printing portion; if sections were undercut, they would break off when printing pressure was applied.

3. GOUGES. Many printmakers prefer the V-shaped gouge (the English call it a "scrive") and the U-gouge to the traditional knife. These tools are available in many sizes to suit the needs of the individual printmaker. The V-shaped gouge may be likened to a tool that renders two simultaneous cuts of the traditional implement when making a white line. Figure II-17 shows how to sharpen the V-gouge if you desire to cut *across* the grain.

Beginning the Print.

At this point, as in all of the mediums of the graphic arts, you are asked to concretize your visual ideas. You may use litho crayon, pencil, brush and ink, or any other device in making the image clear on the face of the plank. If you prefer, trace your drawing on the block with carbon paper and a hard pencil.

Having completed the design on the plank, you will begin to cut out only those lines or areas which you wish to remain white or unprinted. A word of caution at this point. Before the block is reduced to wood splinters, or whenever you feel the need, take a proof of the present state of the block. It may be interesting to keep progressive proofs of your blocks for your records.

Fig. II-17. Resharpening a gouge for use in woodcut.

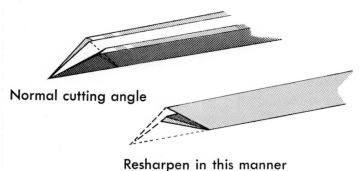

Normal cutting angle

Resharpen in this manner

Materials and Tools for Proving the Block.

Basic tools and materials required for printing or proving the block include an ink slab, printer's ink or oil paint, a brayer, soft rice paper, and a tablespoon or burnisher.

1. THE INK SLAB. This could be a slab of marble about 15 by 20 inches or so, if you can afford such a luxury. A sheet of plate glass would satisfy the requirement as would a too-thin lithographic stone.

2. THE INK. Printer's ink, obtainable from your local print shop or from sources listed in the Appendix, may be used for "rolling up" or inking the block. If the ink is too stiff, especially on very cold days, you may add a drop or two of lithographic varnish to soften it. Ordinary Vaseline (petroleum jelly) will also perform this function, as will artist's oil paint. Use too little of any of these ink-softeners rather than too much for best results.

3. THE BRAYER. The brayer or roller is used for "rolling up" or inking the block. It is usually made of gelatin. Do not allow it to remain for too long on its surface or it may flatten beyond use. When not being utilized in the printing operation, the brayer may be hung on a wall by its handle, so that it is freely yet securely suspended. It may be cleaned with kerosene and then powdered with talc before being stored away. Blocks may also be inked with stiff brushes, a sponge, or a leather dabber.

4. PAPERS. Soft, thin, tough rice papers are best for the woodcut. They allow successful prints with dry paper, though you may damp them if you prefer. It is recommended you try many varieties of paper before deciding upon only one. If you do not have easy access to Japanese papers or local ones, consult the list of paper supply houses in the Appendix. For those who prefer to damp rice paper, here is a procedure that was recently observed by the author. Cut up a newspaper so that it is slightly larger than your printing paper, resulting in a "book" of newsprint. Load a large wallpaper brush with clean water, and pass it over every fourth page in your newsprint "book." Insert several sheets of dry Japanese paper between each wet section. Place the "book" on a large drawing board, then set another drawing board on top of the "book." Weight the top board with a litho stone or some heavy object. In about an hour, the paper should be in excellent printing condition. See other damping procedures in the chapters on Lithography and the Intaglio print.

5. THE BURNISHER. An ordinary tablespoon rubbed over the back of the printing paper when it rests upon the inked block surface works satisfactorily as a burnisher. You may substitute for this a bone or metal burnisher or a Japanese baren, if you can locate one. The baren is a burnishing tool about 5 inches in diameter, slightly convex on the under side, and is covered with a lightly oiled bamboo sheath to allow it to travel smoothly over the paper.

Remove a small quantity of ink from the can with an ordinary table knife. Work up the ink on the slab with a stiff putty knife or its equivalent until it can be manipulated across the slab in a thin film by the brayer. Do not hurry this process.

Now, load the brayer with ink by passing it across the ink slab. Ink the wood block. Do not pass the brayer across and back on the block many times in the same place—this is just wasted motion. All that is required is a thin film of ink, an even film of ink.

Select a sheet from your stack of printing paper and, holding it at diagonally opposite ends, place it so that the completed print is pleasingly spaced on the paper. In order to line it up squarely, check both dimensions of your paper before placing it on the block. After the first few prints, you will always center your paper properly.

Holding the tablespoon so that your fingers are resting in the concave side and your thumb alongside the spoon, briskly rub the back of the paper with this burnishing instrument. If you are using rice paper, the burnishing will allow the image to be seen clearly from the back. If some other stock is used, picking up a corner of the paper from time to time will serve to determine how much pressure is needed for a rich black. Rub evenly all over the paper. Then remove, and stack the prints between dry blotters. Repeat the inking and burnishing for each print in your edition.

After pulling the whole edition, clean the block with solvent. Clean and powder the brayer. Clean the ink slab. These cleaning operations will enable you to do another print, and another, and another without having ruined your tools or your disposition. There is nothing more frustrating than trying to scrape old ink from an encrusted surface; it is even more discomforting to know that carelessness was responsible for your enervating work.

6. PRESSES. There are some printmakers who prefer to print their blocks in a press. While the use of a press is obviously a timesaving device, it is not to be regarded as equivalent to the burnishing method.

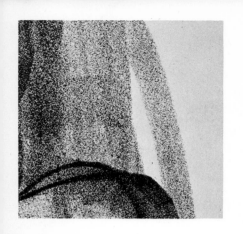

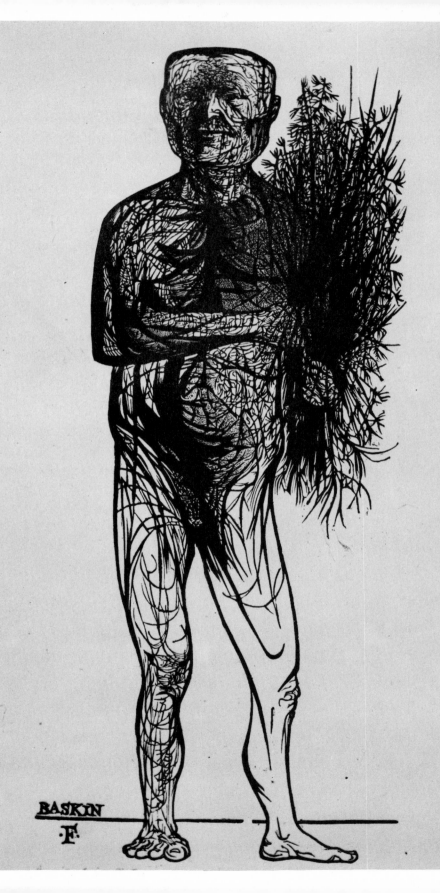

MAKING A WOOD ENGRAVING

The wood engraving is considered by many people to be the draw-ingroom version of its poor relative, the woodcut. However, this nine-teenth-century distinction has little to do with the quality of the compared mediums. It suggests a limited approach to a limitless field. It further suggests a distinction which may formerly have been true, but which has little or no meaning today.

The wood engraving and its traditional white-line, black-ground approach was highly developed, though not originated, by Thomas Bewick. (Compare the illustration of the block itself with that of the print in Figs. II-20 and II-21. The enlargement of the block allows a clear picture of Bewick's every stroke of the graver in the end-grain wood.) This English engraver of the eighteenth century accom-plished the major exploratory work in this particular medium. Since that time the history of wood engraving is replete with cycles of dis-repute followed by others of some popularity. Although today's scene reveals that the wood engraving is a rare phenomenon in an exhibi-

Fig. II-20. Thomas Bewick: "Bison" (the block)

Fig. II-21. Thomas Bewick: "Bison" (the impression)

tion of fine prints, this art form, scarce as it may be, is sometimes an exciting visual occurrence.

Because of the particular tools employed and the nature of the end-grain block, the wood engraving is capable of producing delicate effects or powerful performances, wispy greys or dynamic blacks. Its potential has, by no means, been realized.

Materials and Tools for Cutting the Block.

The basic requirements for making a wood engraving include an end-grain block of wood, many varieties of burins and other engraving tools, and a bench hook or leather pad.

1. THE END-GRAIN BLOCK. For wood engraving, an end-grain block of either boxwood or maple is employed. The latter is about half the cost of the former, though it performs equally well. Sources for blocks may be found in the Appendix. These are type-high (7/8") blocks that are highly surfaced on one side. Turning the block over on the rough side allows you to see the evidence of the labor involved in its

preparation. The end-grain block is employed in wood engraving because it allows you to cut into it in any direction without tearing or splintering.

2. THE ENGRAVING TOOLS. Figure II-22 shows the variety of burins employed in wood engraving. These are classified in many ways. The English system for classification divides the tools into lozenges, spit-stickers, scorpers, and vélos. In reviewing the tools in the same order by a different system, we have the following: standard graver, tint tools, round gravers, and liners or multiple lining tools. All of the tools employed in the woodcut may, if desired, also be used here. All of your burins or engraving tools should be kept well sharpened to allow maximum freedom in use.

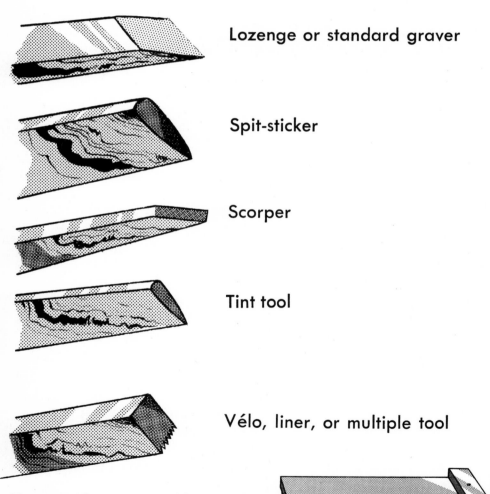

Lozenge or standard graver

Spit-sticker

Scorper

Tint tool

Vélo, liner, or multiple tool

Fig. II-22 (above). Types of burins employed in wood engraving.

Fig. II-23 (right). A bench hook.

3. THE BENCH HOOK. Certain of our printmakers use a bench hook (Fig. II-23) on a tabletop to support the wood block during the cutting process. The bench hook is easily made, as can be seen from the drawing. For those who desire the traditional and expensive rest for the block, it is recommended that they purchase or make an engraver's pad. This is a circular, sand-filled bag that is covered with a good grade of leather. The block is placed upon the pad and rotated as required with your left hand as you engrave with the other. Obviously, there are engravers who use neither bench hook nor engravers pad with seemingly no ill effects.

Cutting and Printing the Wood Engraving.

The burin or graver in your hand should be held in such a fashion that it, in a sense, becomes an extension of that hand as it moves through the end-grain block in front of you. Your gravers produce positive white lines on the black ground that is the present surface of your block—were it printed at this juncture. The image or design you are about to engrave will emerge from the blackness of this block to form a clear, uniform picture, made up of the white lines obtained from your cutting tools. Consider your problem carefully before you engrave.

It may be helpful to darken the surface of the block with a diluted mixture of India ink and water before sketching upon it. In this manner each movement of the cutting tool through the material will expose itself as a white line, or at least a lighter line, surrounded by a dark ground.

It is suggested that you sketch something that is truly meaningful to yourself. The block will offer no difficulties in the cutting process if you will identify yourself with the visual idea to be worked within it. Be secure in your judgment of *what* you will engrave, and the *how* to engrave will grow and mature as you progress.

With the possible exception of a press, the materials and processes are precisely the same as for the woodcut. You may use any press which normally prints material that is type-high. The old Washington hand press is excellent for use in printing wood engravings, in that it is capable of the great pressure needed in securing a good print in this medium.

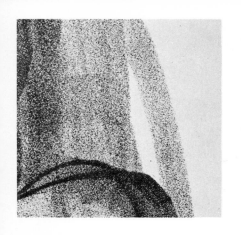

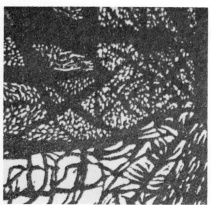

MAKING A LINOLEUM CUT

There is something about even the mention of the word linoleum that seems to make eyebrows shoot upward in disdain. True enough, the particular material under consideration has not always been used advantageously, or (do we dare use the word?) creatively. But, should this deficiency cause us to shun the use of a perfectly adaptable material? Or, should we rather question those who look down their respective noses at this "homely" product?

Obviously, the cost of a piece of battleship linoleum is much lower than boxwood or end-grain maple. This is many times regarded as an advantage by the novitiate. Then, too, the cost of the same piece of linoleum *not mounted on a type-high block* is even cheaper. Purchased in large quantities in a floor-covering establishment, linoleum is inexpensive. So much for the economics of gathering together your materials.

A note may be in order concerning the number of prints possible from a linoleum block. In Mexico City in 1947, the author witnessed an occasion when more than 2500 "pulls" were obtained from a single linoleum block. This is neither to be regarded as a quantitative feat nor a qualitative limitation; it merely points up the fact that this material behaves most admirably.

Beginning the Print.

Although battleship linoleum is available in many solid colors, it is recommended that you purchase white or egg-shell or any high-valued color. It will allow you to work with lithographic crayon and India ink in planning your composition. There is no need to feel hampered or hemmed in by the material with which you are now working. You can cut into the linoleum block in any direction with almost any sharp tool—and in countless ways. Moreover, it is possible to scratch into solid black areas of your drawing, especially if it has been worked with India ink and brush or pen. Scratching *lightly* through the coating of ink with a razor blade or other instrument will expose the white or light colored surface underneath. This factor can be used positively to introduce white lines on a black ground, or negatively to "correct" areas or lines before you begin cutting into the block.

Cutting the Block.

If you desire to make a fine line engraving on linoleum, it is help-ful to scrape the surface thoroughly with the flat of a razor blade and a small quantity of benzine. A few moments of scraping will produce an excellent working surface. Another approach to the preparation of a linoleum surface for fine work is obtained by sanding. Use "wet or dry" sandpaper of the finest grade that can be secured. Sand the sur-face long enough to remove all scratches.

Make certain that your cutting tools are sharp before employing them on the linoleum. Test the quality of the point of each tool by using your thumb nail as the proving ground. If the tool slips when being run over the finger nail, sharpen it until, on another try, it sticks. It is worth remembering that sharp tools dull rather quickly when employed in linoleum, because of the grit contained within the material. Keep them sharp throughout the cutting process both for working ease and the more pleasurable sensations derived from their use. It *is* possible to cut a block with dull tools, but after slip-ping all over the surface and cutting lines you didn't want—both in the block and in your noncutting hand—you will agree it is not a good practice.

Proving the Block.

The printing procedure for linoleum is precisely the same as for woodcut. Ink the block with a brayer and printing ink. Place a sheet of rice paper on top of the inked surface, making sure to center the paper over the block. With a burnisher or a tablespoon, rub the back of the paper sufficiently to bring out the image.

A Few Printing Suggestions.

Gradated color may be applied to your blocks by rolling the color heavier on one side than the other. If you work with a brayer large enough, it may be possible to roll more than one color on the brayer. Obviously, for best results, blocks should be designed with this end in view.

An old practice has been revived, which may prove interesting to contemporary printmakers: An uninked block may be printed in combination with one or more blocks for its textural interest in certain areas. In certain prints, uninked blocks may be employed to pull away ink from already printed areas to reveal an under-printed color.

The *order* of printing colors has much to do in securing particular effects. For example, different greens are produced if yellow follows blue, blue follows yellow, the yellow is wet and the blue is dry, the blue is wet and the yellow is dry, both are wet, both are dry, etc. Try different combinations of the same and different colors to learn their "secrets."

THE RELIEF PRINT IN COLOR

As in most of the other mediums in the graphic arts of today, the use of color in the relief print becomes more and more evident in exhibitions. Many printmakers seem to have forsaken the black and white print for the pursuit of the multiple color block.

The cutting of the blocks is similar to the black and white method, with certain exceptions which will be noted later. It is in the planning stage that the main differences emerge. There appear to be still in practice two basic approaches to the color woodcut. The first conceives the relief print in color as a black "key" block in combination with one or more color blocks; the second suggests that a color relief print is made up of many separate color blocks—no one of them a complete picture in itself—which together make up a complete, unified whole. Obviously, there are wide variations between these two extremes, suggesting that this is a question to be resolved by each graphic artist in terms of his own visual needs. What are some of the color methods employed today? What methods were employed in the recent past?

Color Printing from One Block.

(1) A simple device for the relief print in color was employed by the late Edvard Munch. The design was worked in the wood block by the artist and then carried to a band saw, where it was cut into a set of jigsaw-puzzle shapes. Each of these wooden shapes was inked separately in its own color, then all of them were locked back in their original position, as in a chase for a printing press. The color woodcut was then printed in many colors simultaneously, either by hand

or in a press. The narrow, white line that divides the color areas in Munch's color relief prints shows the quantitative bite of the band saw blade.

(2) This next procedure should be attempted only by those who can foresee and carry out long range plans. Work out a composition in color so that it can be printed in color by a process of subtraction from the same block. Print the whole *uncut* block; or, with a minimum of cut lines or areas, print the block in one color. Pull as many prints of this color as you wish for your edition. Now, remove the ink or paint, and work into the design again, removing more areas from the printing surface. Ink with your second color and print it over the first. Repeat this procedure until you have virtually removed the whole surface of the block, or until you have arrived at a relief print in color which coincides with your original plan.

(3) This is a mechanically easier variant of (2). Work out a complete color sketch for a given size block. Cut a stencil for each separate color you wish to employ in your print. On the *uncut* block, with oil paint and a gelatin brayer, roll stencil #1 on the block. With a second color and a second brayer, do the same with stencil #2. Repeat this for as many stencils as you intend to use. At this point, you will have an uncut block with many wet colors upon it. Place a sheet of printing paper on the block's surface and, with a tablespoon, burnish off the print. Repeat this for each proposed print in your edition. After this is completed, you can use the same block with the woodcut knife and other tools to work your design. Print the completed block over the previously applied colors in another color or black.

(4) Here is a version of the Japanese approach, which may be employed to advantage in one-block color printing. With a stiff-bristle brush, put a few strokes of color (dry pigment plus distilled water) in the area to be printed. Quickly add a tiny bit of rice paste to the same area. Now, with a semi-stiff brush, work the color and the paste together over the required area—rubbing vigorously. Before the color dries out, place a lightly dampened sheet of rice paper on the block, and burnish it either with a Japanese baren or a tablespoon, or a steel burnisher.

(5) Through the use of small gelatin rollers and/or stiff-bristle brushes, separate areas of one woodcut can be inked in different colors. By using oil paint instead of ink, or a mixture of the two, you will be able to burnish this easily with a tablespoon.

Color Printing from Two or More Blocks.

(1) The traditional approach to the color print, whatever the medium, is to cut one block for each color to appear in the final proof. Obviously, this permits wider possibilities than it reads because of potentialities in color fusion or overlay. In this case, a tracing is made of a master drawing for each block to be cut. These are then worked separately and printed separately. To obtain interesting effects, you may try printing the second color before the first is quite dry on the paper. The real problem in color work, however, is the method of registration. There are a number of possibilities for effective registration in the relief print in color:

a. The easiest system, by far, is one that is probably regarded as foolish or dangerous by the professional printer. First, this method assumes that all of the blocks for a given color print are the same size. To attempt this procedure, do the following. Pull a proof from block #1. Now, place that proof face up on a flat, smooth tabletop. Ink block #2 with its color. Turn block #2 wet side underneath, and place it squarely and surely on top of the proof you just pulled. With one hand on the block, and the other one maneuvering the paper from underneath, slide the block and the paper from the table. Holding the paper in place so that it doesn't move, just reverse the position of your hands: the paper now is on top of the block. At this point, you merely have to "spoon" the print, or set it in the press. This process may be repeated as many times as there are colors to print.

Fig. II-26. Japanese technique for registration.

b. Figure II-26 reveals the Japanese woodcutter's approach to the problem of registration. You will notice that a right angle notch and a straight notch are cut on the long side of the block. This allows the damped paper to slide into proper alignment on each block. These notches are cut below the surface of the plank to a depth of $\frac{1}{16}$ inch. Further, you will note that these registration marks are two inches or so away from the edge of the design. Therefore, if you intend to use this method, be sure to select a block that is longer and wider than the body of your design. The "secret" of hairline registration in the Japanese color woodcut, then, is accuracy and craftsmanship. The "key" block is the basis for it all. The registration notches and the linear design must be accurately transferred from the "key" block to every other block used in this process. This may be done by off-setting a wet proof onto a fresh block a number of times. It may be accomplished by precisely tracing the master design on every block. Or, the printmaker may pull as many proofs as there are blocks to be cut. These proofs should be printed on a very thin paper. Remember to ink the registration marks so that they, too, are transferred. Now, paste each proof *face down* on a fresh block. A few drops of linseed oil rubbed on the back of the pasted-down impression will make the black-inked proof transparent. This will allow you to mark out the different areas to be cut with a colored pencil. Do your cutting right through the transparent, pasted-down paper. With careful handling, this should result in highly accurate registration.

c. Two tiny holes drilled in diagonally opposite ends of each color block to be printed provide still another system for registration. These holes should be drilled or pierced in inconspicuous parts of the design. The paper is pierced with a needle that goes into these tiny depressions. To obtain accurate registration, repierce both holes with two long needles. Sighting underneath your printing paper in order to see the block, place the first needle in the proper hole, and then the other. Now, lower the paper onto the block as you remove the needles. Print in the usual manner.

d. Another method for registration of color blocks is achieved in the following manner: Anchor a type-high, wooden right angle to a base such as a drawing board. Have your blocks and your paper standardized and square. Place your registration marks on the outside wooden frame of the right angle, and trace corresponding marks on each sheet of printing paper. Slide your first block tightly into your guide; match the registration marks on your paper with those on the wooden frame. Spoon your print. Repeat for each block in the series.

A variation of this method is accomplished by anchoring the paper to the wooden frame with two strips of decorator's tape or other material. This allows you to pull a complete color print, printing wet on wet, merely by folding back your paper on its hinge. Slide each block in succession into the frame, spoon the color off, and fold the printing paper back until the print is completed.

e. This last method is useful for those who prefer to print a woodcut with the block face down on the printing paper. A Los Angeles printer uses plywood guides with right angle ends and two circular windows for color block registration. His guides vary in size from 3 by 10 inches to 3 by 30 inches depending upon the blocks to be printed.

The guide is placed on the paper, and the registry dots are made with a hard, well-sharpened pencil through the holes in the windows. Now, slide your block into place against the right angle, making sure the inked side is face down. Remove the printing guide without disturbing the "set" of the block or the paper. Apply pressure to print. Now, to print the succeeding colors in your design, place the printing guide back on the paper so that the dots on the paper line up with the tiny holes in the windows. Ink block #2 and place it into position against the right angle of the guide. Remove the guide and print. Do this for each block in the series.

NEW APPROACHES TO THE RELIEF PRINT

The young printmaker of today continues to confound and bewilder his elders in his unusual approaches to materials and techniques in the relief print. Some of these innovations have been brought about through intellectualizing with fellow artists the theory and nature of the relief print. Other avenues for experimental research have been opened up in graphic workshops and individual print studios throughout the world. All of this has stimulated numbers of printmakers to explore the possibilities inherent in new materials and tools—sometimes as an end in itself, sometimes as a better solution to an old problem, sometimes out of necessity.

The average toolshop is one of the most useful sources of instruments capable of "deliberate damage" to the physical surface of the woodblock for the purpose of achieving "new" textures in unusual combination. This repository of "weapons for wood" contains hammers, nails, files, rasps, screw drivers, glue, shellac, etc., all of which may be helpful in enriching the wood surface prior to proving a block.

Experimenting with Unorthodox Materials and Tools.

(1) Cut pieces of wire screen to fit certain areas of your design and pound them into the woodblock surface. Remove and print.

(2) Nails of various sizes may puncture particularly dull areas to enliven them. Entire compositions in the manner of the criblé print may be attempted in this approach.

(3) Cover the surface of a woodblock with glue or shellac and before it dries place various materials on it, such as some cheesecloth, wire screen, a pipe cleaner, string, cord, paper clips, barley, beans, etc. When dry, roll an inked brayer over the parts you wish to print, and spoon off a print on rice paper. A variation on this may be achieved by using a piece of mat board instead of a wood block. This will allow you to make a "collage" in wet shellac. If you have access to an etching press, or a standard press in which type-high blocks can be printed, Charles Smith's experimental techniques may be employed. Ink an uncut block of wood or linoleum that is mounted type high. Place your damped printing paper on the inked block. Now, take your "collage" and place it face down upon the printing paper.

Let us review the position of our elements before proceeding. On the bottom level we have an inked, *uncut* block of wood or linoleum. On top of this a sheet of paper (preferably Japanese) rests. On top of this, and face downwards, we have placed a "collage" (not inked) done on mat board or chip board. When pressure is applied, a print results which is darker where the raised portions exist, and lighter in the cut-out or scraped-away portions. The possibilities of what Mr. Smith calls his "makeready" (collage) technique with other blocks printed in the direct manner seem unlimited.

(4) Substitutes for the woodblock are being employed by numbers of printmakers, especially for color work. Masonite, plywoods, card-

board, chip board, mat board, and other materials are becoming increasingly common.

(5) Various hand tools and small power tools score up surfaces in particular ways. Rasps, for example, leave telltale marks, and a screwdriver jumped across a woodblock makes its tracks. Hundreds of effects are obtainable by the imaginative printmaker.

(6) Relief prints may also be obtained from deep-etched *metal* plates with many interesting variations: (a) Treat the plate merely as an ordinary woodcut in black and white. Ink the surface with a brayer and handle the printing in the normal manner. (b) Printing two colors alternately on the same sheet of paper and deliberately off-registering the second color slightly obtains a most interesting result. (c) Refer to the Intaglio section for still other approaches. These techniques are sometimes called "reverse etchings."

(7) Antonio Frasconi's use of a small repeat block is worthy of mention at this point. This young printmaker has employed, among a number of other useful devices, the technique of a repeat block within the confines of a larger block. Frasconi used this approach in a most inventive manner.

WORKSHOP SOLUTIONS TO RELIEF PRINT PROBLEMS

Problem: You cut a line or area that was not intended.

Solution: Recut the block; or, fill the line or area with wood putty and scrape or polish it to surface height; or, cut out the undesired area and fit a plug of the same material into place.

Problem: When printing the block on a press, certain areas are too light.

Solution: Cut out that area from the print that shows up too light, and paste it down on the back side of the block exactly over the low area. Keep building this low spot up in the the same manner until it prints properly; or build up the overlay until the print shows up evenly.

Problem: In using a press, the print gets darker with each succeeding proof.

Solution:	Too much ink; or, ink too thin; or, pressure too great; or, block of wood too soft; or, paper too dry.
Problem:	In using a burnisher, you cannot get a good black or dark.
Solution:	Use a thinner, tougher rice paper and damp it; or, add a miserly drop or two of varnish to the ink; or, try adding some oil paint to the ink; or, print in oil paint.

BIBLIOGRAPHY: THE RELIEF PRINT

Balston, Thomas, *English Wood Engraving, 1900–1950.* London: Art and Technics, 1951.

Bliss, D. P., *A History of Wood Engraving.* London: J. M. Dent & Sons, Ltd., 1928. 263 pp.

Buckland-Wright, John, *Etching and Engraving.* London: The Studio Publications, 1953. 240 pp.

Chatto, W. A., *A Treatise on Wood-Engraving, Historical and Practical.* London: C. Knight and Co., 1839. 749 pp.

Fletcher, F. Morley, *Wood Block Printing Based on the Japanese Practice.* London: John Hogg, 1916. 131 pp.

Furst, Herbert, *The Modern Woodcut.* London: J. Lane, 1924. 271 pp.

Hind, A. M., *An Introduction to a History of the Woodcut.* London: Constable and Co., Ltd., 1935. 2 Vols., 483 ill.

Lankes, J. J., *A Woodcut Manual.* New York: Crown Publishers, 1932.

Leighton, C., *Wood-Engravings and Woodcuts.* London: The Studio, 1932. 96 pp.

Linton, W. J., *Wood Engraving, A Manual of Instruction.* London: G. Bell and Sons, 1884. 127 pp.

Macnab, I., *Wood Engraving.* London: J. Pitman & Sons, 1947. 53 pp.

Mueller, H. A., *Woodcuts and Wood Engravings and How I Make Them.* New York: Pynson Printers, 1939. 187 pp.

Newdigate, B. H., *The Art of the Book.* London: The Studio, 1938. 104 pp.

Salaman, M. C., *The New Woodcut.* New York: Albert and Charles Boni, 1930. 176 pp.

Smith, C., *Experiments in Relief Print Making.* Virginia: University of Virginia Press, 1954.

Ward, L., *Vertigo.* New York: Random House, 1937. 230 plates.

"While there is copper there is hope."

MAXIM LALANNE

III

The Intaglio Process: Etching and Engraving

INTAGLIO PRINTING has bounced like a man on a pogostick throughout the history of the graphic arts. Currently, it soars, in the estimation of critics and collectors.

Extremist advocates of intaglio claim that it is the most versatile of all graphic mediums, is the sole inheritor of the "Great Renaissance Tradition," and should be practiced by all printmakers to the exclusion of all other mediums. The slightest acquaintance with the visual history of the graphic arts is sufficient to deflate these arguments, but this is not the place for esthetic discussion. No medium in and of itself is per se better than any other.

Granted, the vast amount of experimental work in the field of intaglio tends to influence every practitioner as he, in turn, influences the field and the people who make up his audience. The question of size, despite the unusually large plates worked upon today, is not necessarily settled. The size of a print never was an esthetic or technical criterion. Some in the field tend to work only in black and white, in strong opposition to proponents of color. Others seek eagerly for "accidents" with which to texture their plates and "invent" new visual surfaces to titillate the eyes; still others, being more concerned with their pictorial ideas, allow the image to dictate the "way" in which a particular plate is worked—whether the evolving method is traditional or otherwise. New techniques and new methods may evolve in the conflict of the artist with *what* he has to say; in this manner, the *how* it is said becomes meaningful—not for itself alone, but as visual proof of the necessity for moving away from the strictly traditional approach.

By simple definition, intaglio is an image engraved below the surface of the material. The image on a copper plate from which a print will be taken is incised with hand tools (burins) or etched by acids. The image is filled with ink, and the surface of the plate wiped clean. Damped paper is placed on top of the plate and both are run through a wringer-type press which forces the paper into the channels or grooves to pick up the ink. In a sense, the paper molds itself to the many irregularities cut or etched within the plate. Intaglio, therefore, is a term that describes the printing process by which incised metal plates are printed.

Techniques in intaglio printing are simple enough to be learned in a short while, which is as it should be. It is the persuasiveness of the content and the artist's unity with his visual idea that allows the artist to cut through the technical problems in any medium to produce a work of art.

With these ideas in mind, let us re-examine some intaglio prints from the past and contrast them with a number of contemporary works.

A GALLERY OF INTAGLIO PRINTS—OUR HERITAGE

The world of Albrecht Durer—the intellectual world in which he lived—was a complex, troubled, difficult place in which to survive. In "Melencolia" (Fig. III-1) we sense the unanswered questions, the deep-seated problems, the conflicts and contradictions that beset man in his relations with other men. With all of his tools, inventions, and instruments capable of exact measure, he still searches for new solutions to his problems. Some may suggest that his salvation lies in spiritual fields, as no doubt was intended by Durer. But, is this the only interpretation of this masterwork of engraving on copper? Study of this particular print through a magnifying glass will heighten one's appreciation of the control exercised by Durer in employing his burin to engrave on copper the image burning in his mind. Note the use of the short stroke and the flick or dot that enriches the print surface. The tiny landscape, framed by the ladder, is but one of the many pleasant surprises in the print.

One of the earliest artist's indictments against war was crystallized by Jacques Callot almost immediately after the French invasions of Italy in 1632 and 1633. His "Disasters of the War" (Fig. III-2) was one of a series of engravings on the theme of man's inhumanity to man. Callot also brought to perfection the use of an instrument called an "échoppe," a chisel-edged tool which when turned or twirled between the fingers allowed him to obtain the swelling line seen in the etching of the "Gobbie" (Fig. III-3). Observe the lines on the right thigh and leg of the player. You can almost "feel" the échoppe being twirled in Callot's fingers as he makes each stroke follow the form.

The sweeping landscape of the "Goldweigher's Field" (Fig. III-4) by Rembrandt was obtained through the medium of etching. Contrast the dark accents achieved with the drypoint needle in the foreground and middle ground with the qualities of line elsewhere in the composition. One can observe the velvety or fuzzy edges of the drypoint accents counterposed against the crisp, linear shorthand of Rembrandt's etched line. See how a few strokes in the lower right third of the print define people at work in the fields.

This combination of etching and engraving by William Hogarth brings to life one aspect of eighteenth-century England. In "The Cockpit" (Fig. III-5) Hogarth's biting satire enjoys unlimited freedom; his works stand in direct opposition to the academic portraits so popular in his time. His use of a system of cross-hatching coupled with dots or short strokes seems to grow out of the necessity of the forms he employed. Compare the Hogarth, which uses an overabundance of line, to the Rembrandt (Fig. III-4) which employs so little to create so much.

One of the most imaginative of eighteenth-century etchers was Piranesi, whose fantastic compositions of Roman architectural ruins, real and imaginary, invite the participation of the viewer. "The Prisons" (Fig. III-6) is one of a series of etchings founded upon both knowledge and invention, using Roman architecture and archeology

Fig. III-1. Albrecht Durer: "Melencolia"

Israel ex. Cum Priuil: Reg.

Ces ennemis du Ciel qui pechent mil fois   Font gloire mechamment de piller et d'abattre   Mais pour punition de les auoir brûlez   13
Contre les saincts Decrets et les diuines Loix   Les Temples du vray Dieu d'une main idolatre   Ils sont eux mesmes enfin aux flammes immolez

Fig. III-2 (opposite). Jacques Callot: "Disasters of the War"

Fig. III-3 (right). Jacques Callot: "Gobbie"

Fig. III-4 (below). Rembrandt: "The Goldweigher's Field"

Fig. III-5. William Hogarth: "The Cockpit"

as the point of departure. Piranesi's etched line is a many-sided thing: It varies from the assertive black accents throughout the print to the wispy, tenuous threads in the distance. Seen against the Hogarth (Fig. III-5), the Piranesi etching is a free, airy, light composition.

Fig. III-6. Giovanni Battista Piranesi: "The Prisons"

Fig. III-7. Francisco de Goya y Lucientes: "Disasters of War" (plate 30)

There are other men in the world of art who leave a visual record of their times so potent, so imbued with the drama of life, so filled with rich meaning as to challenge the viewer to respond in kind. Goya was one of the few who left such a heritage to the world.

The empty, vacuous faces of those who would be all-powerful walk ill-at-ease through his prints; horrible monsters and demons fly in brooding skies; the brutality of war is made visible and deathly clear; corruption, vice, love, and hate in a world gone berserk are conjured up before our eyes as we look at his prints; yet, in others there is dancing, music, romance. Goya tells us of the Spain of the Inquisition; Spain with her pageantry of toreadors, matadors, and picadors; Spain of poets, writers, and other intellectuals; Spain of a glorious people; Spain of degradation, poverty, misery. All are brought to life in arresting form.

"Disasters of War" (Fig. III-7) documents the violence and bestiality of war in a series of graphic images that haunt the viewer. Technique, in Goya's work, grows out of the content: There is no separation between the two—no evidence to assume the artist pondered and reflected about which method to employ, or what tool to use. There is a directness of expression linked inextricably to content. Compare this print with that of Callot (Fig. III-2) on the same theme:

Which of the two seems more contemporary in feeling? Why are you a disinterested spectator before one print and a participant in the other? How does the element of time express itself in these prints? What significance, if any, obtains from differences in technique?

Civilization has always had men who, we are told, walk alone; individuals who do not fit into the scheme of things; men who are neglected in their own time for various reasons, but whose work comes to have meaning and even greatness long after their makers are dead. Such a man was William Blake (Fig. III-8), a lonely, poverty-ridden, neglected man who, despite or because of this condition, engraved some of the most imaginative compositions to rediscover engraving as an original medium.

Blake, contending with the difficult task of unlearning old habits, had to overcome the handicap of a hand long experienced in reproductive engraving. Moreover, he invented, through expediency, a method of relief printing from metal plates, and ways of obtaining many colors simultaneously that only recently has been equalled.

This particular plate has been selected as one of the best of Blake. "When the morning stars sang together," one page from *The Book of Job* illustrated and written by Blake, reveals the sweep of his powers, a unity of text and illustration—an entire system of symbols, admittedly complex and obscure but wedded to the realities of his time—a breadth of vision moving beyond the theme of conflict between Good and Evil.

When a man chooses to speak in a language that has little meaning to the vast majority of his contemporaries and when he employs this language in a public medium, he invites inevitable controversy over whether he is sincere, a fool, an opportunist, an over-inflated ego, or any of these in combination. This language and meaning that go beyond contemporary understanding may be forecasts of progress; this is also the way of retrogression. In the work of William Blake we witness a prime example of the former.

Fig. III-8. William Blake: "When the Morning Stars Sang Together"

In "Black Lion Wharf" (Fig. III-9) we obtain a glimpse of the decisive etching line of Whistler. The freedom and fluidity of the etcher's language is clearly demonstrated in this example of the craft. Note the variety of line employed for textural effects in the upper third of the composition. Compare these with the descriptive, lightninglike line of the lower half.

"The Dream and Lie of Franco" (Fig. III-10) by Picasso provides still another approach to the theme of man's inhumanity to man. Since we are dealing with a contemporary, the print takes on even more significance. The horror of war and fascism prompted this combination of etching and lift ground. (See p. 161 for an explanation of the process.) This was not a print done to serve merely as a conversation piece, but one which the artist felt impelled to do because of his complete identification with the content. Why is this print placed in the section of our heritage? The answer to that may be found in many of the new prints being done today—not only in America but all over the world. Whatever one's opinion of Picasso, few would deny his enormous influence upon contemporary art.

Fig. III-9. James Whistler: "Black Lion Wharf"

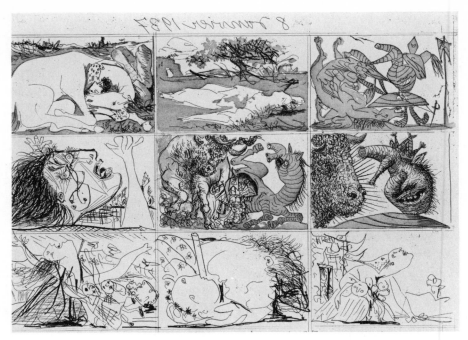

Fig. III-10. Pablo Picasso: "Dream and Lie of Franco"

A GALLERY OF INTAGLIO PRINTS—THE PRESENT

Intaglio prints today look quite different from those of the past. For one thing, size and color contribute greatly towards this "new look." The various influences of the many schools of "isms," the rediscoveries of art forms from anywhere and everywhere in time (a veritable raiding of the art treasures of the past), the ease of communicating reasonable facsimiles of these great works of art, the influence of change all about us in every sphere of man's activities, the artist reacting as a displaced person and taking refuge in his laboratory or studio to find solace in his own experiments—these and other conditions often reduce the artist to an unenviable status. Having nothing to say, and no one to say it to, what is left for him but to experiment some more?

While this may be true or may have been true in the recent past, there are many signs which point to a more optimistic view for American printmaking. The author has heard many printmakers declare that the time had come to stop playing and revelling in experiment for its own sake and move on now to that which is more meaningful, more significant. While these statements in no way have suggested or delimited the *way* in which this would occur (something that couldn't and shouldn't even be attempted), enough has been said by a sufficient number of people to indicate great promise for the future.

The following prints by no means exhaust the range of expression currently going on in print laboratories and studios within the limits of the United States; these are selections made by the author, primarily for technical reasons. Again, it is regrettable but impossible to include all that are worthy.

"Fiddlers" (Fig. III-11) by Walter Rogalski presents us an example of pure engraving on a copper plate. The delicacy and strength, both possible in line engraving, challenge the imagination; the variety of textures and range of tonal values help create a terrifying image.

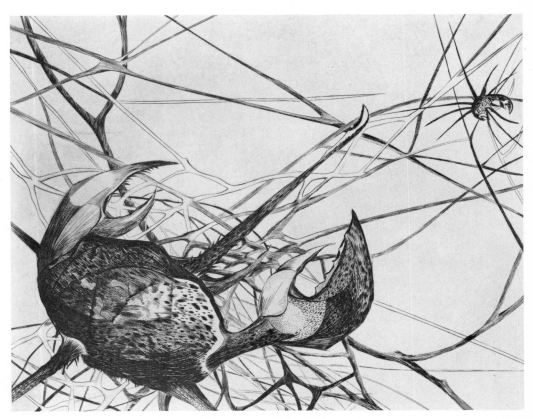

Fig. III-11. Walter Rogalski: "Fiddlers"

"Falling Cock" (Fig. III-12) by Lee Chesney provides a complex technical structure founded upon line engraving and employing etching, soft ground, and aquatint. The textile patterns discernible in several sections of the plate reveal the use of soft-ground etching; the scraper was used considerably in many sections of the plate; the introduction of raised whites which break the picture plane can be traced through Mauricio Lasansky (Chesney's teacher) to Stanley William Hayter. Chesney is an accomplished technician, as is evident even in the wiping of the plate.

The color aquatint, "Surrender" (Fig. III-13), by Vincent Malta lends a three-dimensional note to the intaglio print—solely from a printing device. By superimposing a relief or surface print of his plate (slightly off-register) onto an intaglio version of the same plate, he obtains this curious, rich quality of surface treatment. Color heightens this particular mode of working to enhance the composition.

Harland Goudie exploits the combination of etching and aquatint in "Interior" (Fig. III-14). The luminous values of the aquatint reveal hours of work with the scraper and burnisher.

The entire repertoire of intaglio techniques is evident in "The Firebird" (Fig. III-15) by Mauricio Lasansky. Engraved forms reminiscent of Hayter appear in the upper right of the composition, acting as a foil to the etched lines, bitten surfaces, and burin work to the left. Elements of Picasso, Beckmann, Modigliani, and others appear in the figures and other symbols throughout the print. Lasansky has exercised great influence upon many of our younger printmakers, especially those who work exclusively in the intaglio field.

"Figures of Reflection" (Fig. III-16), a color etching by Leonard Edmondson, is based upon an etched line which both encloses and textures the enigmatic forms. Combinations of soft-ground textures, aquatint, scraping, and other experimental devices (see page 179) provide additional visual interest. Color is applied to the surface by means of stencils overlaid one upon the other after the plate is inked as for normal intaglio printing.

On a foundation of meticulously controlled etched lines in copper, John Paul Jones constructed "Boundary" (Fig. III-17). Soft-ground textures, aquatint, much scraper work, and routing out of the raised white lines combine to form a craftsman's display of the tools at his command.

"Head" (Fig. III-18) by the author is a mixture of soft ground texture with an engraved line. The plate was severely bitten in a strong nitric acid bath; the texture is that of an ordinary pocket comb.

The telling satire and strong social commentary of Harry Sternberg come through in this highly controlled experimental print, "All the News" (Fig. III-19). This combination of aquatint and engraving may not seem unusual, save when one knows that Sternberg used a motor-driven flexible shaft (similar to a dentist's drill) employing a strange assortment of burrs to create the print.

With this brief survey of what has been, and what exists now, let us turn to the technical probems involved in the making of an intaglio print. We shall start with etching and then move through the other approaches in this process.

Fig. III-12. Lee Chesney: "Falling Cock"

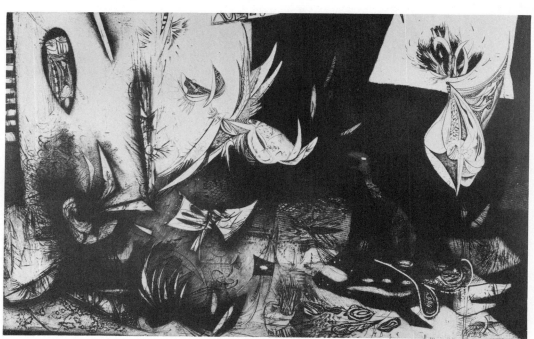

Fig. III-13. Vincent Malta: "Surrender"

Fig. III-14. Harland Goudie: "Interior"

Fig. III-15. Mauricio Lasansky: "The Firebird"

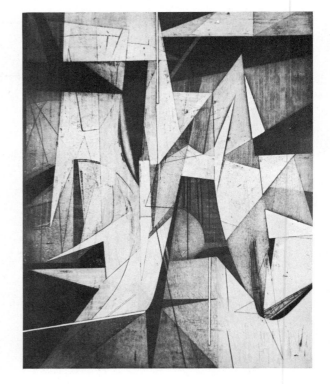

Fig. III-16 (above). Leonard Edmondson: "Figures of Reflection"

Fig. III-17 (right). John Paul Jones: "Boundary"

Fig. III-18 (left). Jules Heller: "Head"

Fig. III-19 (below). Harry Sternberg: "All the News"

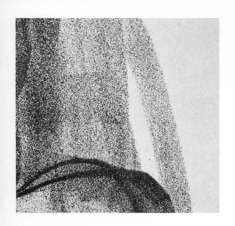

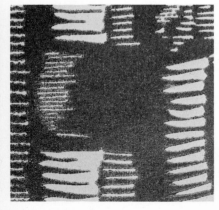

MAKING AN ETCHING

Our first experience in etching is apt to engender a mosaic of emotions, from worry or fear to irrepressible joy. Every etcher, no matter how long he has worked in the medium, can't help but be excited anew at the first proof from a plate. Rarely does the initial proof live up to the artist's expectations: Many believe more was put into the image than comes off on the working proof. Ever present is this element of disbelief in the making of an etching, which may, in some measure, explain the craftsman's ardent interest in the medium. There are many variables in etching which few artists can control consistently. Fortunately, the process allows and encourages reworking to the ultimate satisfaction of the printmaker. Our primary concern is centered on presenting information about the various tools, processes, and mediums which will lead to greater control by the artist, allowing him greater freedom of expression.

The primary principle of the etching problem is to provide the plate with an acid-resistant ground, which will allow the acid to "bite" into the needled design without affecting the unneedled ground. There are many substances which meet this particular need, all of which will be elaborated upon in due course. But, let us first set up a series of requirements for hard etching ground: It should not flake or chip when drawn through with a needle; it should allow being spread to a paper-thin consistency on the plate; it should not soften unduly through indirect heat; it should be dark or black enough to provide a sharp contrast to the needled lines.

The Plate.

The basic material and primary requisite for etching is a plate to carry the etched line or intagliate. A 16- or 18-gauge copper or zinc plate should be purchased from your nearest supplier (consult the Appendix). Though copper is the preferred plate for etching (it allows for finer work, can also be engraved upon, may be used for drypoint, etc.), zinc is also employed despite certain limitations. For example, the molecular structure of zinc is such that engraving should *normally* not be attempted in this material; this applies equally to drypoint. On the other hand, the cost of zinc is usually about one-half that of copper; zinc plates impart a particularly pleasant tone to the final print; for those who require or prefer a "fast" medium, zinc plates react quickly in the acid bath, and are highly regarded by many etchers who work in color. (For additional information on plates see p. 172.)

Today, newer materials enter the arena of etching, though all of them are not necessarily employed in the traditional manner: Aluminum, triplemetal, lucite, masonite, and steel are but a few of the unorthodox substances employed today.

Let us, however, suggest that first attempts in etching be launched in zinc or copper standard gauge plates. You may have to cut your plates to certain sizes in order to have them fit your press; a nearby metal shop can do this inexpensively, if you do not desire to become involved in this aspect of the work.

Cleaning the Plate.

As a preliminary to laying an acid-resistant ground that will adhere strongly on the plate, the plate must be cleaned and free from grease. Omission of this step may cause the ground to break away during the biting. Therefore, with a cotton swab and a mixture of powdered whiting and water, rub the plate thoroughly. (Household ammonia may be substituted for water; any detergent may be substituted for the whiting.)

To test the cleanliness of the plate, hold it under a water faucet and observe the action of the water on the surface of the metal. If it is still not free from grease, the water will form in amoebalike globules. A clean plate allows the water to form an unbroken film over the entire surface. If the latter occurs and the plate is thoroughly clean, dry it by heat on a hot plate or stove.

The Traditional Ground.

Laying a traditional ground is not as difficult or unwieldy as words sometimes make it seem. Nor is it always as simple as one would desire. There is no magic formula for success here—save practice. First, warm the plate on a hotplate and then rub several strokes of hard ground (the traditional ground) about on the plate. (Hard ground, the main ingredient of which is wax, is normally supplied in a balllike shape, about the size of a golf ball.) The heat of the plate melts the ground. Using a leather-covered roller (which you should keep for this purpose only), pass it over the plate in order to obtain an even, thin, protective cover. You may have to go over the plate with your roller in several directions to effect such a ground. If it is too thin or too thick, it will not be acid-resistant or will crack or flake.

Smoking the Traditional Ground.

The traditional etcher smoked his ground both to obtain a greater contrast between the needled copper line and the blackened ground, and to observe flaws more easily. The smoking, neither difficult nor time consuming, is accomplished as follows: Twist several wax tapers together, and line the jaws of a hand vise with felt. Holding the grounded plate face down with the hand vise in your upraised left hand, pass the flame of the tapers across the grounded plate back and forth to allow the carbon to blacken the ground. Do not burn the ground by keeping the flame in one spot too long. When the plate is cool, the surface will be a sooty black.

Rembrandt's Ground.

For those printmakers interested in making their own grounds, we might, in passing, note some that have come down to us through the years. However true or not, Rembrandt is supposed to have employed the following formula: ½ ounce of asphaltum or amber, 1 ounce of virgin wax, and ½ ounce of mastic. These ingredients should be melted together in the given order and allowed to boil up several times. Pour the whole mass into warm water and work it up into convenient-sized balls. You also might cover each ball, after it is sufficiently hard, with a piece of silk so tied as to make a little sack. This will tend to keep dust away from the ground and may prevent unintended pitting during biting. Use this ground as described in the traditional ground.

Transparent Ground.

A simple way to make transparent ground involves weighing out and melting together two parts of wax to one part of gum mastic. Follow the same procedures as for the above grounds.

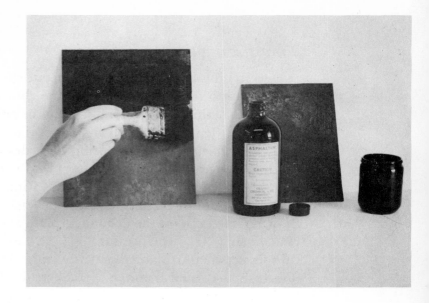

Fig. III-22. Laying an asphaltum ground.

Liquid Ground.

There are some etchers who prefer liquid grounds to all others. Liquid ground is hard ground dissolved in ether or chloroform, dependent upon the particular manufacturer's formula. To use, place a glass rod or wooden dowel rod under an etching tray so that the tray may be tilted easily—like a children's seesaw. Pour the ground into the low end of the tray. Place your cleaned plate, face up, at the other end of the tray and then tilt the tray so that the liquid ground covers the plate evenly. If it does not cover, repeat this procedure. Pour the residue of the liquid ground back into the bottle and cap it quickly. This will keep dust out and stay evaporation of the ground.

The traditional way of using liquid ground is to pour it quickly and evenly down a plate held just off the vertical. The excess is caught in a tray in which the plate is normally standing.

Asphaltum Hard Ground.

Add equal parts of liquid asphaltum and turpentine, and stir well. Stand the plate against a vertical surface and brush on the ground as you would lay a wash. Use a soft-haired brush and place your strokes horizontally, one below the other, covering the plate evenly. Note the manner in which the plate is being grounded (Fig. III-22). The plate should then be heated on a stove to allow the solvent to evaporate and ensure a smooth, even, hard coat.

Transferring the Drawing.

Few etching instructors would encourage the complete tracing of a sketch onto the now-grounded plate, but many will acknowledge the fact that this will be done wholly, in part, or not at all by each individual, dependent upon his particular needs. It may be repetitious to reaffirm this, but tracing does destroy the freshness of the original image. For those, however, who need a method of transfer, these devices may prove useful: (1) Using a cotton ball, rub powdered conte or other dry color onto the back of your sketch. Place the drawing, face up, on the grounded plate and trace the image with a pencil using very little pressure. (2) You may purchase some colored carbon paper and place this, shiny side down, under your sketch. Trace in the usual manner. (3) Sketches done on paper with soft leads may be transferred by damping the sketch lightly with a moist sponge, placing it face down on the grounded plate, and running sketch and plate through the press with less than normal pressure. Use one blanket and a piece of cardboard for this transfer, as in Fig. III-23. This is also effective with images drawn with some ball-point pens.

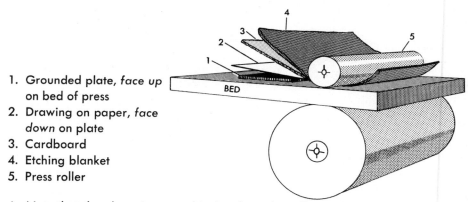

1. Grounded plate, *face up* on bed of press
2. Drawing on paper, *face down* on plate
3. Cardboard
4. Etching blanket
5. Press roller

A. Note that the plate sits several inches from the roller.
B. Also, note that the press roller grips the cardboard and blanket *before* it engages the plate.
C. Pull the bed, under pressure, through the press—*slowly*.
D. Remove the drawing. The image, in reverse, will appear on the grounded plate.

Fig. III-23. A method for transferring the drawing to the plate.

Needling the Ground.

The object of this step is to clarify your visual intent upon the grounded plate with an etcher's needle (a steel tool used for scribing a design on a grounded plate), or any one of a score of substitutes: A darning needle, a dulled dentist's tool, a phonograph needle secured in a pin vise or pen holder, and so forth. Find and use any tool that will both satisfy this requirement and feel comfortable in your hand. You do not need to scratch more deeply where dark lines are intended, as that will be accomplished by the acid or mordant. You *do* have to penetrate the ground and expose the plate.

Preparing the Plate for the First Acid Bath.

Now that the linear aspect of your composition is completed, we want the acid to penetrate only the needled sections at the same time that it ignores the undrawn parts of the ground. The back and the sides of the plate have to be protected with an acid-resist to prevent their being attacked in the bath. The acid-resist, known as "stop-out" varnish, is usually employed for this purpose. It is made quite easily by adding resin to denatured alcohol until you have a saturated solution (in other words, until a sediment begins to form at the bottom of the vessel). Stop-out can be thinned, therefore, for easier brushing on the plate, by adding denatured alcohol to obtain the desired consistency. Paint the back and the sides of the plate with a soft brush loaded with stop-out. Some etchers use straw-hat polish, stove polish, asphaltum hard ground, and other substitutes.

When brushing stop-out on already bitten lines to prevent further attack by the acid, be certain that the entire channel is filled with the resist and that the edges of the line are equally protected. Remember to wash the plate well with water and dry it thoroughly before applying stop-out between different bitings.

Use of Acetic Acid.

Some printmakers bathe the needled plate in acetic acid prior to the actual biting. This procedure is recommended because it removes all traces of grease from the lines to be bitten and allows the stronger acids to bite equally all over the plate. You need not wash the plate after the acetic acid bath; merely slip it into the stronger solution after it seems clean.

Acids for Etching.

There are not too many acids currently in use by etchers. Perhaps this is as it should be. Most common are nitric acid, hydrochloric acid, potassium chlorate, and iron perchloride. The following table (Fig. III–24) may be helpful in selecting the proper mordant for a particular job. In actual practice, you may find one acid that will serve most of your needs. There is no need to utilize all of these formulae.

Fig. III-24.

TABLE OF ACIDS FOR ETCHING

Acid	Plate Zinc	Plate Copper	Formula	Gas Generated	Effect
Nitric	×		1 part nitric acid 6 parts water *	Hydrogen	Bubbles—bites horizontally as well as vertically; broad, irregular lines; bites *much-needled* effects faster than single lines; tendency to undercut.
Nitric		×	1 part nitric acid 3 parts water *	Nitric oxide	
"Dutch mordant"		×	⅕ oz. potassium chlorate in 5 oz. *hot* water. Add 1 oz. hydrochloric acid.	Chlorine gas given off when *mixing* the solution. Do not breathe the fumes.	Bites straight and deep lines; no bubbles; lines darken during biting.
Iron perchloride		×	To a saturated solution of iron perchloride, add an equivalent quantity of water.	None	Bites clean, even lines. Sediment of iron oxide forms in lines, slowing down biting. Plate should be bitten upside down—an obvious disadvantage.
Acetic acid	×	×	Use 30% solution.	None	Merely employed to remove grease from needled lines prior to biting.

ACID COMBINATIONS TO OFFSET DISADVANTAGES

Iron perchloride *plus* 10% hydrochloric acid		×		Dissolves iron oxide sediment in lines.
Nitric plus iron per- chloride (noncritical in amount).		×		Stays tendency to widen lines.
Dutch mor- dant plus ni- tric (enough to create bubbles).		×		Allows you to "see" foul biting immediately, due to bubbling action.

* More or less water can be used, dependent upon the strength of the bite desired. For a slower etch add more water; use less water for a faster one.

FIRST AID

1. Flush acid-exposed area immediately with water or weak solution of ammonia.
2. Apply bicarbonate of soda (baking soda) to neutralize acids.
3. Call a physician.

Biting the Plate.

The plate is lowered into the acid bath (mordant). The etcher may wear rubber gloves or may run a string under the plate to aid in lowering it, as in Figure III–25. Through the years, etchers have developed three major approaches to biting the plates, plus a host of individual variations upon the dominant themes. The first approach stems from a completely needled plate which is bitten and "stopped out" as many times as desired by the artist. In other words, after a minute or so the lightest passages are prevented from further biting by coating them with an acid-resist or stop-out (e.g. a saturated solution of resin in denatured alcohol). The plate is then returned to the acid bath and this procedure repeated until the final darks are achieved.

Fig. III-25. Lowering the plate into the acid.

The second approach starts with the needling of the darks first. The plate is submerged in the acid bath and biting takes place. The lighter and progressively lighter lines are needled as you proceed. In actual practice, both of these approaches are usually employed. When you want to cross heavily bitten areas with light lines, it is obvious that you should take the second method. The English etcher, Haden, carried this approach to an extreme in submerging the grounded plate in acid and then, *when it was under the acid*, he would needle in his dark lines, doing the entire plate without removing it from the acid. This method had a certain spontaneity which was greatly appreciated in Haden's time.

The third method involves using a feather or brush to carry the acid over a partially needled design. It sometimes incorporates what has been called "spit-biting." Saliva brushed on a grounded plate will confine nitric acid to that particular area. It is normally employed to obtain washlike effects. At this point, it might be well to mention one historic method of biting a plate without an acid tray: A wall of wax is built up from under the plate to make a shallow vessel, and a lip may be fashioned at one corner to allow for easy pouring of the acid back into its container. Acid is then poured onto the surface of the plate and held within the walls of wax.

Controlling the Biting.

If you use a bath of nitric acid for your plate, you will notice bubbles of nitric oxide or hydrogen gas forming in the lines—the former if your plate is copper, the latter if it is zinc. These gas bubbles appear almost immediately. If not removed from time to time, the bubbles prevent the acid from further attacking the plate.

Removal of the bubbles from time to time is accomplished in one or more ways. The older generation recommended employing a feather for the job. Some suggest a pipe cleaner; others advocate the use of a chinese brush, while recent experts suggest doing nothing more than tilting the bath tray sufficiently to expose the plate to the air. The last suggestion is based upon the desirability of keeping foreign objects and articles out of the acid bath.

When biting a copper plate in a nitric bath that seems sluggish, especially if it is freshly mixed, add either some old mix (blue from the copper sulphate in solution) or drop a penny into the bath.

Do not intermix nitric solutions for zinc and copper, unless you are prepared for or desire uncontrolled and unpredictable effects. For example, if you place a needled zinc plate in a bath of nitric acid which had formerly been used for biting copper plates, you would achieve nothing more than copper-coated zinc lines and a poor bite. Obviously, such intermixing is good practice to avoid.

If you are using a bath of iron perchloride, it may be helpful to bite your plate face down in the bath, supporting the plate on small pieces of glass rod. This procedure will allow the black copper oxide to fall to the bottom of the acid tray, keeping your lines clean. If the plate is bitten face up, you have to stop and remove the deposit from time to time to allow a uniform bite.

Acids are quite temperamental; their behavior varies from place to place, subject to many variables over which artists have little or no control. The confirmed etcher regards this as part of the excitement of the total process, and looks upon it as a compensation rather than a disadvantage.

How long should a plate be bitten? "Longer than you think" is the answer of experience. Repeated observation of beginning etchers reveals that most of them fail to allow the acid to penetrate deeply enough into the plate. In their own terms, they are usually dissatisfied with the first bite. This may be avoided by (1) making a test plate;

or, (2) setting up an arbitrary geometric progression for line depth in minutes of biting time; or, (3) direct observation of the process in the hands of a seasoned craftsman. The most satisfying answer to the above question is that which derives from your own experience with the materials. The inconstancy of acids reacting to age, temperature, the particular hardness or softness of the plate, etc., challenges the printmaker to exert his utmost in controlling this medium.

When removing the plate from the acid bath, tilt the acid tray so that the mordant runs down to the bottom. Pick up the plate by two corners, with or without rubber gloves, and wash it immediately with water. Dry the plate with paper towels or between blotters before examining it.

Remove the ground and stop-out with their respective solvents (turpentine and alcohol) and clean the plate thoroughly. Some etchers prefer to scrub their solvent-soaked plates with sawdust in a large wooden box set aside for this purpose.

PRINTING THE INTAGLIO PLATE

The printing of an intaglio plate is as much a part of the total process as is any other step. If a group of first-rate photographers were given the same anonymous negative and each was asked to make a print from it, the resultant prints would show a general resemblance —yet each one inevitably would reflect certain individual differences. Similarly, if a number of printmakers were requested to pull a print from someone else's plate, each printmaker would inevitably leave the stamp of his own personality upon it. The prints would, once again, resemble each other, but only as do siblings their parents— if that much.

Consider the problem at hand: We now have a plate that has been scored, roughened, cut, scraped, burnished, rocked, rolled, needled, or bitten with acids. Our purpose is to obtain a print from this plate. To do this, we fill all of the pits and depressions with ink, leaving the surface of the plate clean. We then place a sheet of soft, damped paper on top of our inked plate and run it through a wringer-type pressure of hundreds of pounds per square inch. This action forces the paper down into the lines, pits, and depressions, allowing the ink to appear in relief above the paper surface when it is pulled from the plate. We will have taken a cast of the lines and other hollows in ink on paper. Looking at the back of the print, we can see the depressions in the paper; turning the paper over, we can see the lines standing up in relief. Now, let us examine the intaglio printing process in greater detail.

The Press.

The action or principle of the etching press resembles that of the old-fashioned clotheswringer, save that it has a heavy bed that rides through the two rollers under great pressure. In addition, we can alter the squeezing pressure of the rollers for optimum results by turning two pressure screws (see Figs. III-29, 30). There are many variants of this principle that have been manufactured throughout the years. Some of these presses have substituted a half-round top roller (D-Roller press); many are geared for easier manipulation; others are ungeared. For driving the bed through the squeezing roller action, the handles vary from simple, straight, single rods, to many handles (star wheel), to the large wheel seen on geared presses. Some presses are tabletop, portable models; others are floor type affairs that weigh well over a ton. Despite the many differences in handles, weight, price, size of rollers, width of bed, and presence or absence of gears, all are similar in principle. Portable models and all presses having a top roller under six inches in diameter are regarded by many experts as being mere toys. The larger the diameter of the top roller the finer, more qualitative the print will be. However, this does not mean that good proofs cannot be pulled from the smaller presses; many printmakers do remarkably well in proving their first works on equipment that seems something less than desirable.

The Blankets.

The blankets used in the printing of an intaglio plate are expensive, resilient rectangles of piano felt. Since the finest grade of felt is used in good printing, these blankets should receive excellent care; this will reflect itself in consistently qualitative proofs.

The texture and quality of the blanket nearest the plate directly affects the "look" of the print; this face blanket or fronting should be thin, close woven, malleable, and yet possessed of a degree of elasticity. The other two or three felts (each printmaker uses his own number of felts for his "perfect" prints) may be *thicker* than the face blanket, but should possess the same attributes.

Blankets should be washed in soap and warm water at the slightest tendency to harden. Blanket rigidity, caused by absorption of the size in printing paper, is often the cause for poor printing. Every workshop should have two or more sets of blankets to cope with this mechanical problem. Through alternation and repeated washing, this difficulty can be eliminated.

Adjusting the Press Pressure.

Though few printmakers are called upon to put a press together, you may at some time or another find it necessary to set or reset the press pressure in order to pull a proper print (see Figs. III-29, 30).

To begin with, pull or roll out the press bed. Place the fine felt blanket (the thinnest one) on the press bed so that it is flat and evenly lined up with the bed edges. Place the next two or three blankets down upon the first one, stepping them back to allow their going under the top roller easily. Tighten the pressure screws by hand and turn the press handle to allow the blankets to travel under the roller. You may have to push the bed with one hand as you turn the handle with the other. Make certain, as soon as the blankets are gripped firmly, that they have not twisted or wrinkled. When the blankets are under the roller an inch or so, stop turning and throw the blankets up and over the roller.

Now to test for plate pressure: Take an already worked but uninked plate and place it face up between a clean, folded blotter. Pull back the felts one at a time, straightening and smoothing each of them in turn. Then, pass the bed through the press by turning the handle. When you feel that you are off the plate, and before you override the blankets at the end of the bed, stop the press, throw back the blankets over the top roller and examine the raised white-on-white impression made by the plate upon the blotter. Tighten or loosen one or the other pressure screws until the impression appears perfectly even; check the plate marks around the sides as well as the impress of the plate itself. A makeready may be needed for a particular area that prints poorly in an otherwise perfect plate. This can be done simply by isolating the area on successive proofs, cutting out the particular area and pasting the cut pieces of paper down on the back of the plate, printing and repasting until you are satisfied with the image.

If you own your own press, chances are that you would do this once and never disturb the pressure except for hairline adjustments on certain work. When working a press used by a group, adjustments may be necessary if allowed by the individual in charge.

Bevelling the Plate.

To prevent the sharp edges of the plate from cutting the blankets or the printing paper, it is important that you bevel the edges of your plate with a fine-toothed file. Round the corners and polish and remove any scratches on the edges before printing.

Inking the Plate.

Warm the plate upon the stove and put a small quantity of ink on the plate's surface. With a hard roller kept only for this purpose, or with a tightly rolled piece of felt (called an "ink rubber" by some, or a "dabber" by others—see Fig. III-26) roll or spread the ink firmly over the plate so as to force the ink down into the lines, pits, or depressions. If you can still see shiny places of copper, you have not inked the plate thoroughly. Keep rolling until you are certain all the intaglio work is filled with ink. (See pp. 141–142 for a more detailed discussion of inks.)

Wiping the Plate.

Tarlatan pads are recommended for the wiping procedure. These pads are made up by folding and refolding a yard of tarlatan until you have a 5- or 6-inch circular wad that is flat on the bottom. Keep these wiping pads in three separate piles so that you have one group that is heavily coated with ink, another that is less so, and a third that is suitable for the final wiping, where a clean pad is necessary. On plates other than drypoints and mezzotints you may cut matboard discards into 3- or 4-inch squares to use as squeegees in removing some of the excess ink before wiping with a pad.

With a rather firm pressure, start wiping the plate briskly with the oiliest of your tarlatan pads (Fig. III-27). It is recommended you wipe in circular or arclike movements. Make certain the bottom of the pad is flat so that it does not take ink out of the lines. As the plate becomes less obscure, switch to a less oily pad and continue to wipe, using less pressure. The amount of pressure to be used and how clean to wipe a plate—whether to use *retroussage* (an enriching effect obtained by flicking a piece of cheesecloth over a clean-wiped plate to get the ink to "spill" slightly over the lines) —all of these must be determined by the individual printmaker in terms of the specific print on which he is working.

Use cleaner pads and less pressure as you proceed; hand-wiping may be employed to obtain a faint, silvery, brilliantly clean look. Rub the heel of your palm on a chunk of whiting; brush off the excess whiting and wipe the plate with the heel of your palm. Be sure to clean the edges of the plate before printing.

Fig. III-26 (left) . Inking the plate.

Fig. III-27 (right) . Wiping the plate.

Fig. III-28. Placing the printing paper on the plate.

Pulling the Proof.

Warm the clean-wiped plate on the stove. Check the bed of the press for cleanliness to keep the margins of the print free from stains. Some printmakers place a thin sheet of zinc on the bed as a protective covering; others use a fresh sheet of newsprint each time, or a blotter; some merely wipe the bed clean each time with a soft rag and solvent. On a clean bed, then, place the warmed plate, face up. Take a sheet of damped printing paper and, holding it at opposite corners as in Fig. III-28, place it over your plate decisively. A clean sheet of newsprint or a blotter (or nothing at all) may be placed on top of the printing paper. Referring back to the section on blankets, we see that the best texture for printing is cloth and not paper. Pull each blanket down over the plate and paper without disturbing their relative positions (Fig. III-29), and smooth down each blanket in turn. Roll the bed through the press very slowly and evenly without stopping (Fig. III-30). Throw up the blankets; carefully "pull" the printing paper from the plate by slowly peeling it from one corner. Examine the proof carefully before pulling another one. Does it need corrections, additions, alterations? Is it satisfying? Before attempting to answer these questions, let us stretch our proof.

Fig. III-29 (above). Pulling the blankets down over plate and paper.

Fig. III-30 (right). Running the bed through the press.

Stretching the Proof.

On a plywood or masonite panel, tape the damp print with butcher's tape exactly as you would stretch a sheet of watercolor paper. Overlap the top edge of the proof by at least one-half inch with your brown tape. Pull from the bottom of the proof as you tape that edge to the board. Now, tape the other two sides. The prints will dry flat, and may be removed by cutting with a razor blade.

Some printmakers dry their prints by stacking them between damp blotters, slipsheeting each print to keep it from offsetting. The stack of drying prints should be weighted and the blotters need to be replaced continually with new ones as drying continues. The prints should be perfectly flat in a day or two.

Damping the Paper.

There are two main developments or schools of thought on the damping of paper. The first is mentioned in the chapter on Lithography; the second approach suggests submergence of each sheet of paper in a trough or tray of water for an optimum time (Fig. III-31). The length of time is obviously dependent upon the particular kind of paper employed by the printmaker. As there are hundreds of varieties in use, this question is answered solely by the authority of individual experience. When ready for use, the paper is taken out of the tray one sheet at a time and the surface moisture is carefully removed by blotting. Place the wet sheet between a sandwich of two blotters and rub carefully on the top one until all of the apparent moisture is gone. Leaving wet spots would cause the ink to be repelled from that particular area.

For recommendations on papers for intaglio printing, see the Appendix.

Inks and Ink Making.

Though there are a number of sources for purchasing ready made ink for intaglio printing (consult Appendix), many printmakers prefer to mix and grind their own ink. The advantages to making your own ink are practically self-evident: The economic saving is enormous; you *know* the ingredients of the particular ink and can

Fig. III-31. Softening the paper for intaglio printing.

alter them for each particular problem; there is greater control possible with your own mix.

Here is one formula for ink: Black pigments should be purchased from a reliable supply house, as the quality of the pigments cannot help but influence the final result. Frankfort black, vine black, and ivory black make a good trio of pigments for the beginning inkmaker. To 5 parts of Frankfort black, add 1 part each of ivory black and vine black. Mix the powdered pigments well. Then add plate oil (heavy) and a little *raw linseed oil*. Work up this mixture until it is firm, at which point it should be ground with a pestle on an ink slab.* Do not add too much oil at first (this is the usual error that produces an ink too liquid). Grinding, of itself, takes care of that problem. Keep mixing the ink until all traces of grit are gone. If the ink is mixed in a fairly clean environment, it might be left on the ink slab to age for a while before being stored in airtight cans or tubes. After working in the field for a while, you no doubt will experiment with variations of your own.

* An old lithographic stone may serve as an ink slab; a marble slab, porcelain, or a sheet of plate glass will also be useful if it has been roughened or sand-blasted.

Reworking the Plate.

An examination of your first proof while it is stretching flat on the wall may reveal the need for further work upon the plate. If the idea still is not visually clear, if the need is felt for the addition of values or certain textures to enrich the idea without resorting to visual embroidery, if the linear pattern needs correction, addition, strengthening—all of this and more may be accomplished, provided we know what we want to do and, perhaps, why we want to do it.

Study your proof as it dries on the wall. Would you like to work into it with charcoal, pencil, or white chalk to make your visual intent still clearer? The additions of these materials or others on the proof will provide a guide when working on the copper plate.

For those who desire to contain their print within the boundaries of etching, their problems may center about ways of regrounding the plate both to rebite certain lines and to etch new ones. Regrounding a plate is at best a highly skillful, rarely successful enterprise; at worst, it spells disaster. However, it may be attempted in one of the following ways: Heat the plate in the normal manner and roll on the hard ground with a very stiff roller. This may not fill in the lines you desire to rebite. Another method employs the grounding of an *un-worked* plate first, and transferring to your plate by offsetting one upon the other. Still another approach consists in packing all of the bitten lines with something that would "lift" from them were the plate regrounded in the normal manner and submerged in the acid. Casein paint would be useful in this regard. Remember to clean the surface of the plate thoroughly before regrounding. A final approach may be made by regrounding the plate with transparent ground and reneedling each line to be rebitten.

For those who wish to add values, textures, and other linear qualities to their plates, the following pages in this section provide sufficient information to stimulate the printmaker to his own solutions.

The Scraper.

The scraper is a most valuable tool in reworking certain passages, in cutting deeper lines, in removing other lines, in shaving away whole areas of the copper plate, and in other ways still to be realized. It is a 3-sided steel knife set in a wooden handle and kept razor sharp

Fig. III-32. Employing the scraper.

for use. It is recommended that you tape the upper end of the instrument to protect your fingers when using it. Keep it sharp by working all of its facets with the finest of emery paper. While it should not be thought of solely as an "eraser," which lends to the tool a certain negative quality, this particular function cannot be overlooked or slighted. When the study of your proof leads to the conclusion that it is necessary to remove a given area from the plate, use the scraper, holding it as close as possible to the plate surface to actually shave away the unwanted copper (as in Fig. III-32).

If or when this is carried too far, the depression in the plate may be so great as to warrant hammering up the back of the plate to effect a level surface once more. This may be accomplished in one of two ways: Either use a calipers to outline accurately on the back of the plate the particular area that needs hammering, and do so on an anvil or other heavy, level surface; or, take several proofs and cut out the unpleasant area from the proofs. Paste these up on the back of the plate in their exact relationship to the particular area. Run the plate through the press, and the thicknesses of paper will force the plate level again.

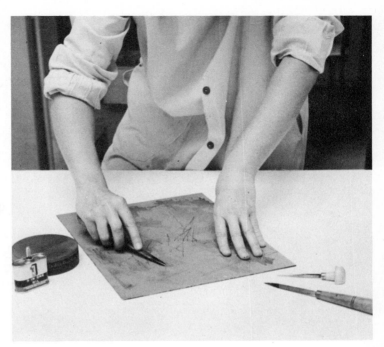

Fig. III-33. Employing the burnisher.

The Burnisher.

This is another useful tool with which to smooth over minor lines, lighten areas, diminish textures, etc. It is a highly polished, smooth, steel instrument that should be used with a little machine oil for best results (Fig. III-33). The burnisher should not be allowed to rust or become pitted. As with all of your tools in engraving, they should be kept in excellent condition. When any of them are not going to be used for a while, it would be well to grease them with a little petroleum jelly.

MAKING AN AQUATINT

At some time or other in your initiation into printmaking, the desire to add values in broad areas becomes great enough to make you want to do an aquatint (see Figs. III-13, 14, and 17). Here again, the principles and techniques are simple, while the mastery of the medium and its integration with meaningful expression may challenge you for life.

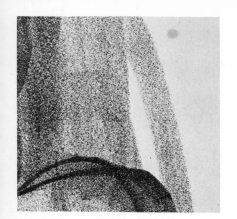

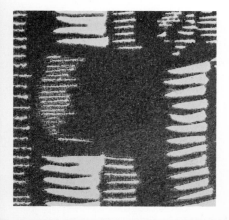

Since aquatint is also an intaglio process, how is it possible to obtain variations in value over broad areas which range from white to black, and which may require hard or soft edges at their respective perimeters? Figure III-36 shows a cross-section of an aquatint plate which clarifies this problem. Powdered resin particles are dusted onto the surface of the plate. When the plate is heated, the resin particles melt and each of them becomes an acid-resistant dot or blob. The acid pits the area surrounding each particle of melted resin and creates a cavity that will hold more or less ink dependent upon the length of the bite. Multiply this individual performance thousands of times on one plate surface, and it is evident that by stopping out white areas and by different lengths of biting time, etc., different values are obtained. In addition, the quantity and the coarseness or fineness of the resin laid on the plate also determines the quality of the "grain" on the surface.

Fig. III-36. Visual explanation of aquatint.

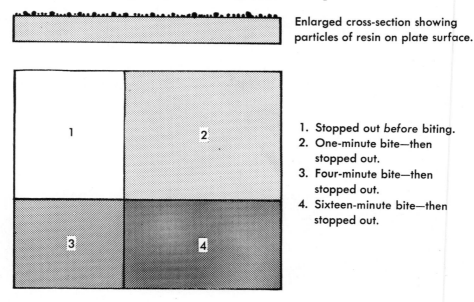

Enlarged cross-section showing particles of resin on plate surface.

1. Stopped out *before* biting.
2. One-minute bite—then stopped out.
3. Four-minute bite—then stopped out.
4. Sixteen-minute bite—then stopped out.

Applying the Resin Grain.

There are a number of ways of applying the resin to the plate surface. Any one of them alone or in combination may be employed. Use the one that seems most responsive to your approach to the medium:

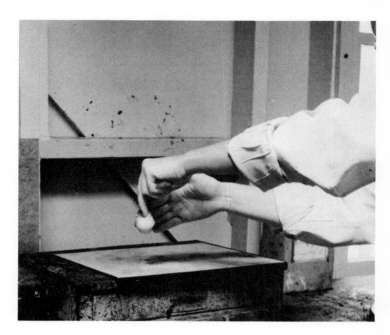

Fig. III-37. Dusting resin on the plate.

1. RESIN DUST GROUNDS. *a.* Place about five tablespoons of powdered resin in a 5-inch square fragment of a nylon stocking, tying up the ends to make a small bag. (The resin may be purchased in lump form and crushed through a used household meat grinder to the consistency desired.) Now, move to an area of your work place where there are no drafts. Hold the bag of resin about 6 inches over a well-cleaned plate and tap the bag gently with a pencil or your other hand as in Fig. III-37. The resin will fall to the plate and cover the surface evenly if you move the bag slowly over the area above the plate. How much resin should you shake out? Too much and too little resin on the surface will result in a coarse grain. At an optimum point, when about 40 percent of the surface is evenly covered, a fine grain is achieved. Being careful not to bump the plate or in any way to disturb the resin particles on the surface; place the plate on your heater or stove. The whiteness of the resin will slowly turn colorless as the plate heats up; you will soon see the plate color clearly; the surface of the plate will look as though it holds thousands of tiny droplets. Move the plate to the bed of your press and allow it to cool. At that moment when it is cold, it will resemble a sea of frozen beads of perspiration. You must be wary of both underheating and overheating your plate. Signs of overheating will be evident to your eyes and

nose. To test for underheating, rub the palm of your hand firmly over the now cold resined plate. None of the resin should powder off in your hand.

b. For a more mechanically perfect grain, you will need to construct a simple dusting box, though it can be as complex and elaborate as you care to make it. In principle, finely powdered resin is placed in a large airtight, lightweight box and the resin is set in violent motion, either by shaking the box or by forcing a stream of air through a small opening into the box. This last may be accomplished either by a hand bellows or a small powered fan. After a moment or two for allowing the heaviest particles to settle, a clean plate is placed at the bottom of the box for a certain period of time—experience will answer this question in more specific terms. The plate is removed carefully, and heated as before.

Fig. III-38. Employing a liquid resin ground.

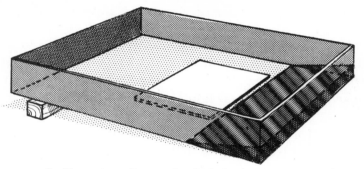

1. Tip-up tray. Pour resin-alcohol solution in one end. Place plate in bottom of tray as shown.

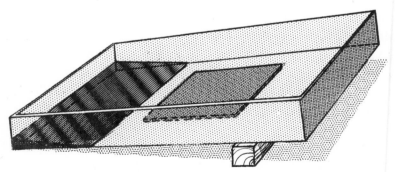

2. Tip tray in opposite direction. Ground will cover plate. Repeat until satisfactory results obtain. Pour remainder of solution back into bottle to prevent evaporation.

2. LIQUID RESIN GROUNDS. These are the older methods, which take a great deal of experience to manipulate. Make a saturated solution of resin in denatured alcohol. Now, take that solution and use it in varying amounts of denatured alcohol until you obtain a ground which pleases you. To apply it to a cleaned plate, here is a simple method: Fig. III-38 shows how to apply the resin-alcohol solution to the plate. Upon evaporation of the alcohol, the resin particles will be affixed to the plate. A purely experimental texture results if the plate is heated before evaporation takes place. I might point out that very few printmakers today utilize the liquid resin ground method; it seems to be too highly temperamental an approach.

Biting the Aquatint.

Since more of the plate is exposed to acid than is covered by the melted resin, it follows that we should use a milder etch than is normally used for ordinary solid grounds. Dutch mordant and iron perchloride, being mild in action, are preferable acids for this purpose. If nitric acid is used, it should be diluted with water to slow down its usual boiling action. With stop-out varnish, other than resin in alcohol (since alcohol is the solvent for the ground), carefully paint out those areas you wish to remain white. With the exception of one print of Goya's wherein no line whatever accompanies the aquatint, it is rather expected to see the bitten line in company with aquatint. The linear etching, then, is done before adding the aquatint. Stop out the sides and the back of the plate and immerse the plate in the acid bath. Remove after a minute or two (or less, dependent upon the strength of the acid, and the depth of tone you desire). Wash the plate thoroughly with water, then dry it. Now, paint out those areas you wish to remain light gray. Rebite, and continue this process until you obtain your blacks.

Three questions come to mind at this time. (1) How can you get a soft edge? That is, how can you make an aquatinted area merge imperceptibly with an adjacent area? (2) How long should the plate be bitten to get a variety of values? (3) If you underbite certain areas, is your work ruined?

(1) a. The use of a litho crayon worked up to the edge of a stopped-out area will serve to soften an edge. If the black crayon is gently gradated from dark at the edge of the brush stroke to white at the

opposite point, you will have achieved a soft edge. *b.* By gently blowing on the acid bath in a tilted tray, you can avoid a hard edge. *c.* Placing the plate in a tray of water that just barely covers the surface of the plate allows you to drop or swab or brush full strength acid in local areas. The edges will be quite soft as the acid radiates outwards.

(2) The length of the bite for specific values in aquatint can best be determined individually by each printmaker in terms of his experience with the medium. Some sample plates worked up in the author's print laboratory have required from a few seconds for a very light grey to 1 hour for a dark. The next week, with the same bath, it took 2½ minutes and 3 hours to obtain the same values.

(3) If a plate is underbitten, there are some remedies that may be tried. One is to reground the plate with a *finer* resin ground than was used the first time. Another is to ground the plate with bitumen powder instead of resin. A third approach suggests rolling hard ground with a firm roller over the surface of the heated plate. When it cools, place it in the acid bath after the necessary steps are taken as for any plate.

The scraper and burnisher may be used to great advantage upon an aquatinted plate. Very little effort is required to lighten passages here in aquatint (a tonal medium), as compared with linear approaches in etching or engraving. Some men have gone as far as biting a plate to extreme blackness (imitating the mezzotint) and then burnishing and scraping out the middle and light areas as they proceeded.

Other Tonal Grounds.

1. SANDPAPER AQUATINT. After having grounded a plate as for etching, it is possible to achieve an aquatintlike surface in this manner: Place a sheet of sandpaper face down upon a grounded plate which lies on the bed of your printing press. Using less pressure than for printing, run them through the press. Removal of the sandpaper will reveal many tiny holes in the ground. Turn the sandpaper and repeat the process a number of times. Too much pressure will force the sand grains into the plate and damage any white areas intended thereon. Too little pressure will leave the ground unpenetrated.

2. SALT AQUATINT. Before removing a grounded plate from the

heater (when using hard ground or soft ground), sprinkle the surface evenly with ordinary table salt. The salt will penetrate the hot ground and affix itself to the plate. After cooling, the plate may be placed in water so that the salt dissolves, leaving the metal exposed.

3. SPRAY TECHNIQUES. With a diluted solution of resin in denatured alcohol it will be possible to run the gamut of house and garden appliances in obtaining tools for spraying stop-out on the surface of a plate. From the common toothbrush technique to the spray possibilities of the vacuum cleaner, there are a variety of instruments at one's disposal.

4. "MANIÈRE NOIRE". Starting with a hard-grounded plate, a dulled needle, and an accurate straight edge, rule parallel lines as close together as is possible without breaking down the ground (having the ground chip). Do this in four directions. When the plate is bitten in the acid and printed, the result, provided none of the ground breaks away, will be a midnight-black surface. Work on the plate with burnisher and scraper to bring your image out of the darkness.

A variation, less mechanical than the ruled approach of "manière noire," consists in passing a wire brush or a finely-toothed comb over a hard-grounded surface in the pattern desired. If not overdone, this can be quite effective.

5. OFFSET GROUNDING. Heat a cleaned plate upon your stove; take any coarse material or flat, textural object which has been thoroughly coated with hard ground, and pat it on the heated surface of the plate. The ground will, of course, offset onto the warmed metal. Stop out those portions of the plate not to be bitten in the acid, and proceed to work in the usual manner.

MAKING A SOFT GROUND ETCHING

Closely related to etching, this particular variation employs a ground that does not harden. The ground for this approach is easily made by melting down a ball of hard ground to which you add half again as much of automobile cup grease, Vaseline, tallow or mutton fat, lamb fat, etc. The acid-resistant material thus obtained will never harden, so that almost anything deliberately pressed into the ground will remove its equivalent of the ground to expose the metal. It then can be bitten in acid as an ordinary etching.

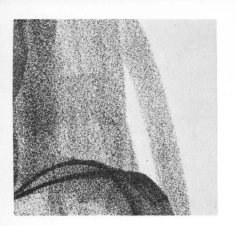

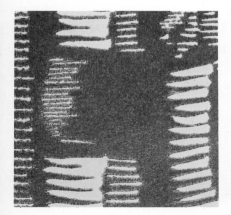

Laying the Ground.

The traditional manner of making a soft ground etching is done as follows: Heat the plate, as is normally done for etching. Rub on a good quantity of the soft ground, and roll it out with a leather or hard rubber roller to be used solely for this purpose. Remove from the hot plate before it burns and continue to roll as the copper plate cools. When finished, the plate should be a definite brown color. If it is light or high in value, chances are that the ground is too thin to withstand the acid bath for very long. The ground need not be smoked in this approach.

Composing upon the Plate.

Figure III-41 explains the principle involved in this approach to printmaking. A sheet of paper is placed or stretched across the soft-grounded plate and a drawing or tracing is made, rather firmly, on the paper. By picking up a corner of the paper from time to time, you will observe how much pressure your pencil must make on the paper to penetrate the ground and expose the metal.

Fig. III-41. Traditional method of soft-ground etching.

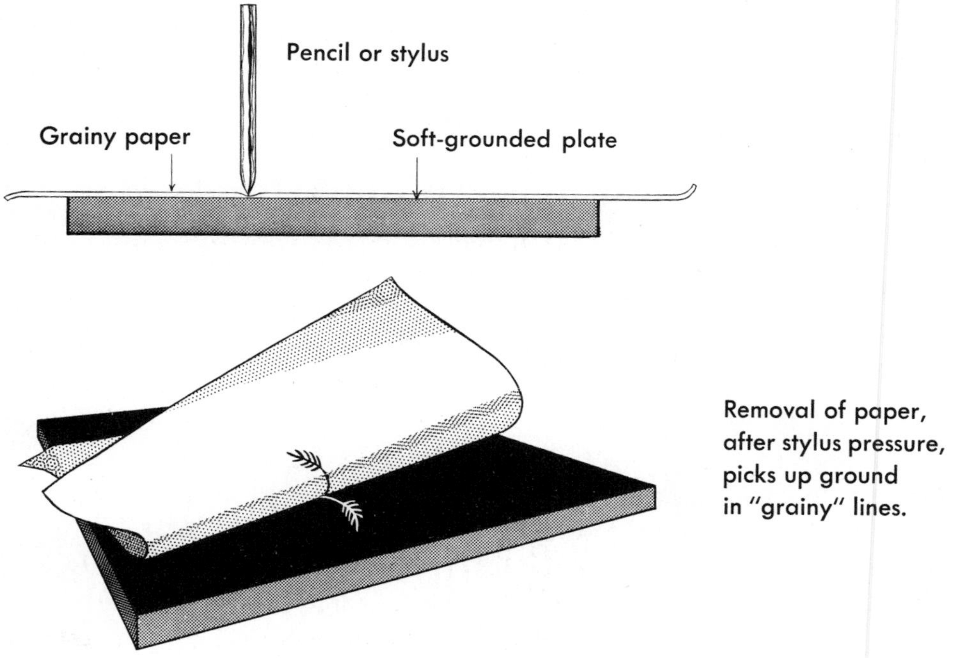

Pencil or stylus

Grainy paper

Soft-grounded plate

Removal of paper, after stylus pressure, picks up ground in "grainy" lines.

We see, therefore, that the grain and weight of the paper and the specific pressure employed by the artist upon his pencil or stylus fashion the granular or lithographic "look" of the soft ground etching. Upon closer examination of the lines in a traditional soft ground etching, you will find them to be made up of many irregular dots and globs—similar in many ways to a soft pencil line on rough paper.

You may stretch your tracing or a fresh sheet of paper across the plate, fastening it with tape on the back of the metal as you do when stretching a sheet of watercolor paper. Damp your paper thoroughly before doing this. When dry, it will be wrinkle-free and ready to receive the weight of a pencil or stylus point.

Recent usage of soft ground etching suggests that contemporary printmakers have done away with this indirect approach and have employed this medium primarily as a textural device in a complex format. For example, direct and indirect impressions upon the soft ground are made with string, lace, net, fingerprints, and other materials too numerous to mention.

Etching the Plate.

The biting of a soft ground plate proceeds in exactly the same fashion as does normal etching. Again you have three major approaches: The plate can be bitten from dark to light, from light to dark, or from area to area by moving the acid around with a feather or pipe cleaner.

Reworking the Plate.

After examining your first proof, and this is the point at which you bring to bear upon the problem all of your resources, you no doubt will make changes. You may want to build up certain textural areas that presently look dull and uninteresting. Certain sections of the plate may have been overbitten; others may seem too weak. Work, then, upon the proof with chalk, litho crayon, or any other combination of materials that allow you white to black, and boldly set about altering the composition with your scraper and burnisher. Keep copies of the various states of the work as you proceed. These will be invaluable as reference material for your future work—especially if you make notes of particular problems and solutions.

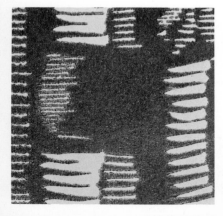

LA ♀ TRUCHE

MAKING A LIFT GROUND ETCHING

Here is a method of painting with brush and a sugar solution upon a plate, covering the whole with a liquid ground, yet magically being able to immerse the grounded plate in a bath to once more view those brush strokes on the bare copper. Aquatint or soft ground are laid in the open or lifted areas and the plate bitten in acid. This process is usually repeated for other values which are added to the design.

In aquatint, a brush stroke of stop-out on a grained surface would later show up in the print as a light figure against a darker ground. The artist who wants the figure bitten, rather than the ground, avoids aquatint like the plague, unless he really enjoys stopping out the whole ground. But our man who likes to see his brush strokes as dark figures against lighter grounds would do well to take up lift ground. Note how Picasso employs lift ground with etching in Fig. III-43. Each brush stroke is a dark or positive stroke—the opposite of aquatint.

Many printmakers have experimented with lift grounds for years, and most of them seem satisfied to use the one developed at Atelier 17 by Hayter, as follows: To a saturated solution of sugar, add India ink to color the mixture and allow it to be seen. Add a small quantity of liquid soap to relieve the textured quality of the brush stroke. Paint this on a cleaned plate and let dry.

Ground the plate with a liquid ground. Let this dry. Then, immerse the plate in warm water fairly soon after the last step. Since the sugar really doesn't dry completely, the ground above it remains porous. Water seeps in, swells the sugar solution, and forces it to "lift."

If you have laid a ground that is too thick, you are in difficulty. Nothing will seem to lift. At this point, you may try adding some acetic acid to the warm water bath, or with a soft brush try gentle rubbing over the parts that are supposed to lift. If this fails, do it all over again.

In the lifted areas you may now lay an aquatint ground or a soft ground. Before biting, parts of these may be stopped out. The biting action may be strong, weak, or in-between, dependent upon the final effect desired. If the composition is made up of several values, the whole process may be repeated for each new grey in the print.

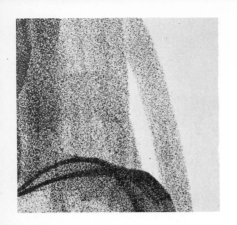

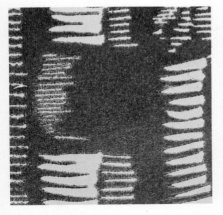

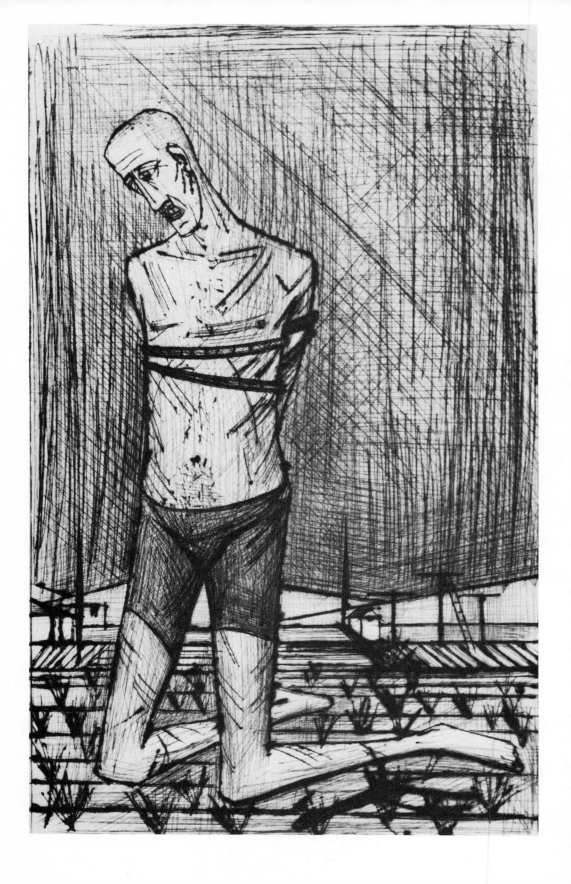

MAKING A DRYPOINT

Drypoint is one of the most tenuous mediums within the graphic arts. From a purely objective viewpoint, it may seem difficult to understand that mere lines scratched into a copper surface with a sharp needle—just scratches, mind you—present great difficulties. Perhaps the answer lies in the fact that there are no visual "stunts" between the image and the spectator; there is nothing but the artist's almost naked intent clothed merely in the rich velvet line of the drypoint.

The needle, in the hands of the artist, ploughs furrows in the copper plate much the same as does the farmer in tilling the soil. The furrow or "burr," as it is called in drypoint, is the distinguishing characteristic of the medium. This ridge of metal catches and holds ink in the wiping of the plate for printing, and it is this factor that makes the lines in a drypoint seem soft and warm. The individual lines themselves are much shallower than those in etching and engraving, and possess but little character should the burr be removed by the scraper.

On a bare plate with a needle in your hand and an idea to express, you work to clarify your visual intent.

Materials.

The needle or point can be purchased or made by the printmaker himself. Best results are obtainable with a diamond point mounted in steel and set in a suitable holder. Ruby, sapphire, carbide, or steel points are equally popular; reground dental tools, engineers' scribes, pin vises with steel points, etc., fill the needs of other printmakers.

The plate may be zinc, but copper is preferable both for the greater number of prints to be obtained as well as for its working properties. Brass, aluminum, steel, and numbers of plastics also may be used. Celluloid drypoints are not recommended even for practice, as they in no way reflect the possibilities of the medium.

The suggestion of the main outlines in your drawing may be made on the plate with litho crayon, if the surface is shiny; with ordinary lead pencil, if you have deliberately dulled the surface; or, it may be transferred to the plate by damping the sketch (pencil or ballpoint pen) and running it through the press face down on the plate. It is not advisable to try to follow slavishly the outline or tracing on the

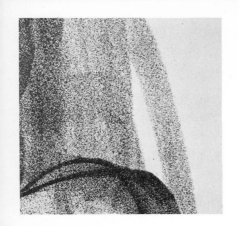

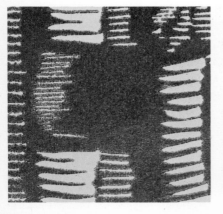

plate; to do so would impose a quality not to be sought for—an abundance of conformity.

In cutting with the point or needle, you will find that it takes a rather strong pressure to obtain a forceful line. There will be no difficulty whatever in accumulating many minor and unwanted scratches. Much has been written about particular ways of holding the drypoint needle in order to achieve certain lines; yet, long observation leads to the belief that this should be discovered by the printmaker himself. It is a rare and wonderful pleasure to see a contemporary printmaker produce a good drypoint.

On reworking a drypoint, you will use your burnisher and scraper —most probably, only the burnisher.

MAKING A LINE ENGRAVING

Man seems to have an irrepressible urge to incise images into hard, intractible materials. In Paleolithic times, perhaps the longevity of the picture thus created possessed for him a magical quality; in depicting an animal, for example, the visual symbol would not only "capture" the animal—a most important consideration in an economy dependent upon both food gathering and the hunt—but would serve to aid man in his struggle with Nature. The unity of the traces cut in Old Stone Age times suggests that early man held a profound understanding of the visual world around him. Contrary to popular opinion, these traces are not crude, ill-fashioned approaches to naturalism, but masterly evidence of realism shouting the triumph of man over his environment.

Engraving may be defined as the act of cutting or incising grooves or channels into a plate, block of wood, or any other material which will "hold" the trace. When these grooves are filled with ink, and damped paper is forced into violent contact with the plate, the resulting *impression*, strangely enough, is also called an engraving. To further confuse the issue, recent use of the term "engraving" includes all of the mediums of the graphic arts in which the artist is his own designer. In this chapter, and wherever else used, we will delimit the word "engraving" to mean both the act of cutting into a plate of metal with burins, and its resulting impression on paper.

In this sense of the word, then, line engraving does not go back before the first half of the fifteenth century, when it was developed by goldsmiths. Yet, even here, engraving was done primarily for the decor of the metal. It was not until the year 1446 that the first dated engraving appeared.

The need for a precise image that may be delicate or bold, "intellectualized" or wildly expressionistic, simple or complex, may lead us to the medium of line engraving. Given an idea, then, which literally drives us to seek, discover, and experience this particular craft, we can only suggest or hint at some of the problems and considerations along the way. This is so truly different from any of the other mediums in the graphic arts that personal trial, for the printmaker, is almost a necessity for evaluation. The crisp, clear, powerful line of Fig. III-11 (p. 115) is worth study at this point, before going on.

Materials Required for Engraving.

Here again, we have a minimal set of requisites: one or more burins, an India oil stone, a metal plate, scraper, burnisher. Other incidental requirements are cited in context.

Fig. III-48. Side and front views of burins.

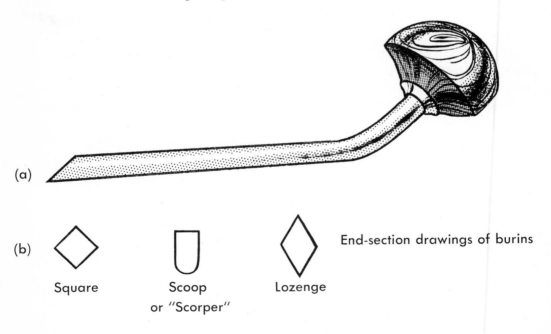

(a)

(b)

Square

Scoop
or "Scorper"

Lozenge

End-section drawings of burins

1. THE BURIN. This innocent-looking tool (Fig. III-48a) or deadly weapon, as you choose to regard it, is the nucleus of the engraving. This is not to suggest that proper care and feeding of this little monster results in its doing your thinking for you on the copper plate. Nor is your task made easier if you allow your burins to dull, become haphazardly ground, or covered with rust.

This hand tool appears in a variety of guises. As the end-section drawings in Fig. III-48b portray, some are lozenge-shaped—excellent for fine line work; others are square-ended—best all-around tool for contemporary use; still others are rectangular save for the rounding of the cutting edge (scorpers)—used for hollowing out deep trenches in the copper.

The act of engraving leads from exasperation to frustration for the worker who uses blunt tools. It is no less trying to attempt a particular line on the plate, only to find that you have cut another because the tool slipped, or the point broke. Sharpening the burin, once you have acquired experience performing this task, is a simple act. First, check the two undersurfaces of the tool to make certain they are knife-edged at their juncture, are parallel to the axis of the steel rod that is the tool, and reveal two unmarred facets or planes all along the length of the instrument. If this test is not met, the undersurfaces of the burin should be sharpened in the following manner:

On a sharpening stone such as carborundum, place the burin flat on one of its undersurfaces. Holding it *firmly* in place, draw it up and down the stone sufficiently to "true-up" the surface. Repeat for the other undersurface. Finish the grinding on an Arkansas stone or the equivalent. This aspect of sharpening may not have to be done at all or possibly once, dependent upon the particular tool you have purchased.

The cutting facet normally needs constant sharpening as you proceed in making an engraving. For this, use an India oil stone #1B64 Norton list, or other circular stone. Hold the tool as close to the cutting point as you find comfortable, making certain it is perfectly flat on the stone. Keeping your wrist rigid, in order to maintain a flat edge, rotate the tool on the stone; a flexible wrist during sharpening will create an ovoid or spherical facet. Again, finish by honing the burin on the fine side of your India oil stone, Arkansas stone, or equivalent. In testing the sharpness of your burin, hold the tool in your right hand, and place the point of the cutting facet on the thumb-

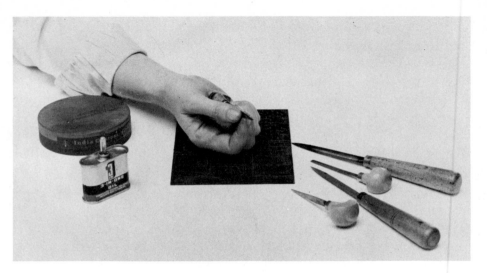

Fig. III-49. "Natural" hold for the burin. Hand is turned over to show grip.

nail of your left hand. If the tool sticks as you push it, it is sharp. If it slides and scratches your nail, it is dull.

There are many treatises on engraving which insist upon the "proper" way to hold the burin when cutting. With due respect to such authority and experience, it seems that there are too many variables, physiological and otherwise, to reassert this dogma here. Suffice it to say that each man will find his proper way of holding the tool by merely observing his own hand as he picks up the burin from the surface of the table. It is suggested, therefore, that what seems "natural" to use is correct. Figures III-49 and III-50 point up this statement in visual terms.

2. THE PLATE. Sixteen-gauge copper is recommended for most line engraving. This is not to suggest that one cannot engrave on other materials or on other thicknesses of copper. Lucite, steel, 18-gauge copper, and other materials have been used successfully. It is a matter of personal choice, quite related to one's pocketbook.

While hammered copper is most preferable to all others, its cost is such that few engravers will indulge themselves. When copper is hammered (and this is a *hand* process), the molecular structure of the metal is altered in such a way as to harden the plate. It is desirable for line engraving that this over-all hardness be present in the plate.

Most practitioners will probably use rolled-rod engravers' copper, both for its availability and cost. The surface of this plate, and of all copper plates, is so mirrorlike and brilliant as to tire the eyes and, in addition, to discourage tracing or transfer. To offset this disadvantage, the surface should be deliberately dulled. Dip the plate in a mild acid bath, or scour it with fine pumice and water.

At this point, a sketch may be made with pencil directly upon the dulled plate. Tracing may be accomplished with black or colored carbon paper from an already completed drawing. Complex drawings which require accuracy could be transferred in this manner: Coat the plate with a mixture of gum arabic and water (a thick mixture). Trace the drawing or the main lines of it upon the gummed plate through carbon paper, after the gum is dry. With an etching needle, scratch through the gum and into the plate without using too much pressure. Remove the gum with water and proceed to engrave.

Fig. III-50. The act of engraving.

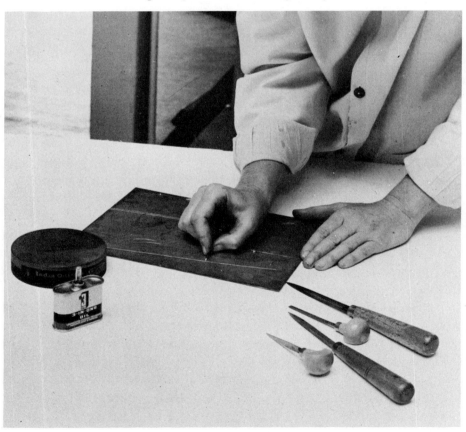

Cutting the Plate.

Some suggestions may be appropriate at this time concerning the physical act of engraving. Since this is not a medium for the quick sketch, and since it involves many hours of cutting, it would be advisable to check your physical surroundings. Does the light reflected from the plate still glare in your eyes? Can you turn the plate easily and smoothly on your work table? Do you seem to tire quickly?

Though many contemporary engravers frown upon the use of a filtered light screen in front of the window at which they may be working, you may find it useful to stretch a large sheet of tracing paper on a wooden frame for mounting on the window. Or, experiment with the light (artificial) or light source to find the right combination for your own use.

An engraver's pad, a luxury mentioned earlier (see the chapter on Wood Engraving), may allow for easier rotation of the plate. On the other hand, any smooth work surface allows your left hand to turn the plate when engraving curved lines or circles.

You might stop and analyze your engraving position or posture, if you tire rapidly. Most craftsmen find it satisfactory to sit sideways or parallel to the side of the work table, with the engraving arm flat on the table. The plate should be just below the eye, on the edge of the table. The burin should be held in as relaxed a manner as possible. Pressure, therefore, will be supplied by the shoulder, the palm of the hand, or by the successive impulses of the plate pushed by the noncutting hand. If the angle of attack of the burin upon the copper plate is too great, all the force you can muster does little or nothing in advancing the burin in the metal. Hold the burin so that its point can enter the copper easily and smoothly; this is done by lowering the angle of attack, or, stated another way, by holding the burin as closely as possible to the surface of the plate. Once the burin is travelling easily in the copper and is removing the metal from the trench, the slightest variation in the position of the hand will be reflected in the trace. The line can swell, go deeper, become a mere wisp of a movement, or a veritable ravine, dependent solely upon the idea of the printmaker and his sensitivity to his materials.

The burin in the hands of an artist is capable of an infinite variety of visual possibilities. Although this instrument has been employed in countless ways, you can use it as a means for obtaining your own personal expression. Experiment with this tool; find out what it can do for you; make it an extension of your innermost ideas.

MAKING A MEZZOTINT

Of all the mediums within the field of graphic arts, the mezzotint has had more than its share of abuse heaped upon it. Since its inception in the seventeenth century, there have been very few practitioners of the art who might be regarded as originators. For the most part, the mezzotint has been regarded as a medium for translating oil painting into a cheaper, more widely distributed print. Artists, in the main, regarded this field as one for the reproductive craftsman only and maintained a cold distance from its laborious demands. As we shall see, however, there is little reason to ignore the medium from the standpoint of its potentialities for the creative mind.

A mezzotint is not unlike a drypoint in that the entire surface of the plate is composed of thousands of burrs. As Davenport* suggests, looking at the surface of a mezzotint plate through a microscope "resembles a choppy sea suddenly solidified." This "sea" of burrs is put there by using an instrument known as a "rocker" (Fig. III-51).

* Cyril Davenport, *Mezzotints* (New York: G. P. Putnam's Sons, 1903.)

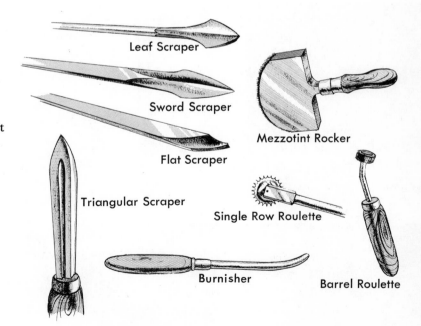

Fig. III-51. Mezzotint tools.

Leaf Scraper

Sword Scraper

Mezzotint Rocker

Flat Scraper

Triangular Scraper

Single Row Roulette

Burnisher

Barrel Roulette

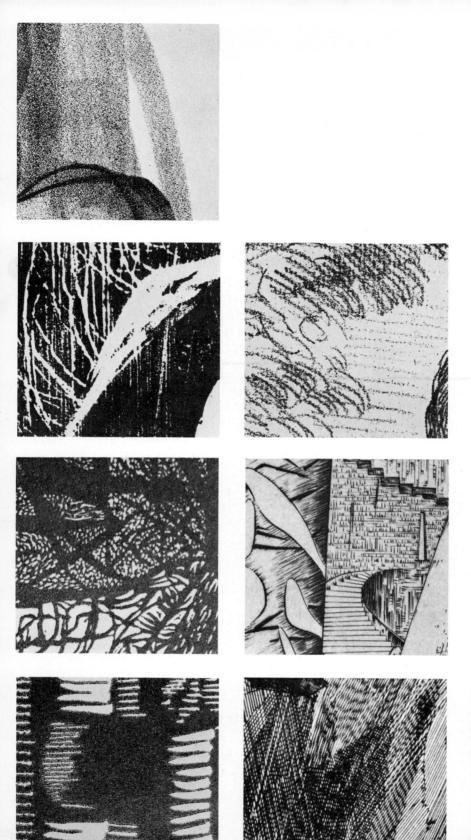

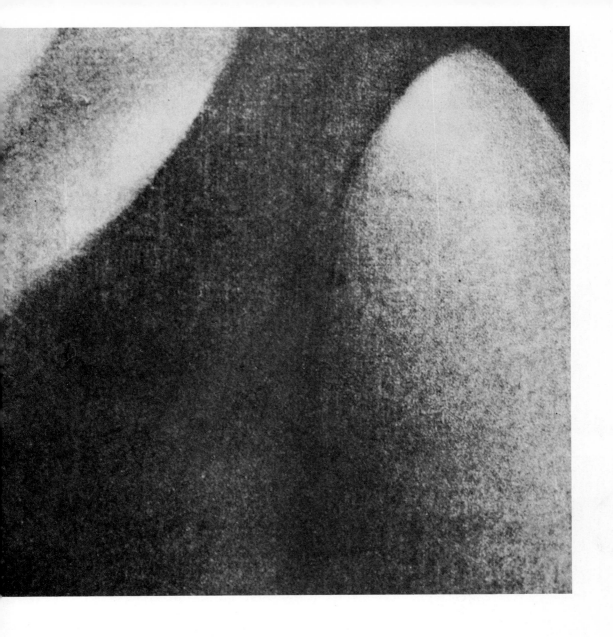

This tool is literally rocked from side to side, digging its teeth into the metal plate as it creeps onward throwing up a surface of burr. This rocking motion is carried out from many directions, fully realizing Davenport's description.

When the plate is finally grounded, work begins with the scraper and burnisher. The former will remove the burr from unwanted areas, the latter will merely flatten it somewhat. The process runs from dark (the grounded plate) to white (a scraped and burnished section). Roulettes (see Fig. III-51) are used to rework or reburr certain scraped areas. The variety of scrapers suggests some of the possibilities inherent in the medium.

WORKING IN MIXED MEDIUMS

On the basis of much visual evidence, the printmaker of today delights in mixing mediums*, especially in the intaglio field. Although he has acquired a vast number of controlled techniques, no one of these individual approaches serves to satisfy his insatiable desires or demands upon the copper plate. The burin, needle, roulette, etching, aquatint, soft ground, deep etch, and relief printing are all intermingled upon and within the plate to make it—the plate itself—a most pleasant object to view.

"Presentation" by John Paul Jones (Fig. III-55) provides an excellent source for the artist about to embark upon a series of trials in the use of mixed mediums. The basis of the print structure stands upon the crisp line of engraving. But, within this structure the artist has utilized soft ground, drypoint, etching, aquatint, and deep etch to enrich and fulfill the print. Study the detail of this print (Fig. III-54) to note the order and discipline of Jones' approach.

Perhaps more than any other individual, Stanley William Hayter may be regarded as the man who most influenced the recent course of printmaking in the United States. Figure III-56, is pure Hayter both in technique and in concept. The powerful, sweeping lines of his burin play in counterpoint with the aquatint and soft ground textured forms; these, in turn, form the ground upon which raised white accents poise above the picture plane. This is an excellent example for study. The new printmaker will observe here, as in all of the examples

---

* The word "intaglio" is often substituted for "mixed mediums" by practicing printmakers.

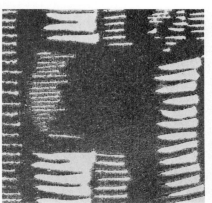

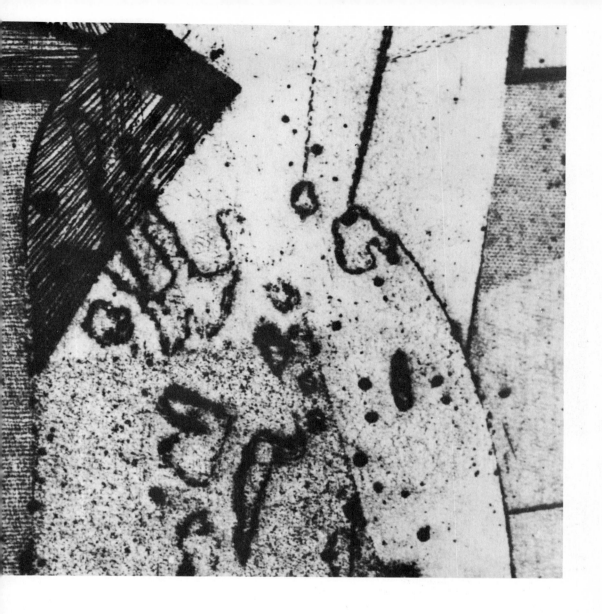

selected, the fine craftsmanship and sensitive performance of this leading graphic artist.

Another avenue open to the experimental-minded is found in the deep-etch and relief print in color, "Noel," by Sam Kaner (Fig. III-58). Here, a certain freedom and flexibility in the use of acids is required, as well as a certain assurance or security in the art of printing. Kaner demonstrates these traits in his work as he seeks to move in new directions. A study of a detail of the print (Fig. III-57) reveals the use of both hard and soft rollers employing different colors.

The reader is invited to look back at Figures III-12, III-14, III-15, III-16, III-17, III-19 to compare and contrast the handling of mixed mediums by different artists. Is line or value the dominant motif in the print? What intaglio mediums have been used in combination? Are those that have been employed in specific prints "at home" with one another? Or, do they "fight" with each other? These questions, to be at all useful, must be answered by each individual for himself.

Since the vast majority of contemporary intaglio prints leans towards a greater, freer use of *color* than has heretofore been true, let us analyze this new field in some detail in the next section.

Fig. III-56. Stanley William Hayter: "L'Escoutay"

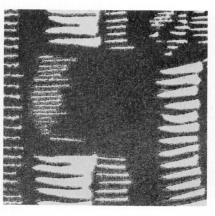

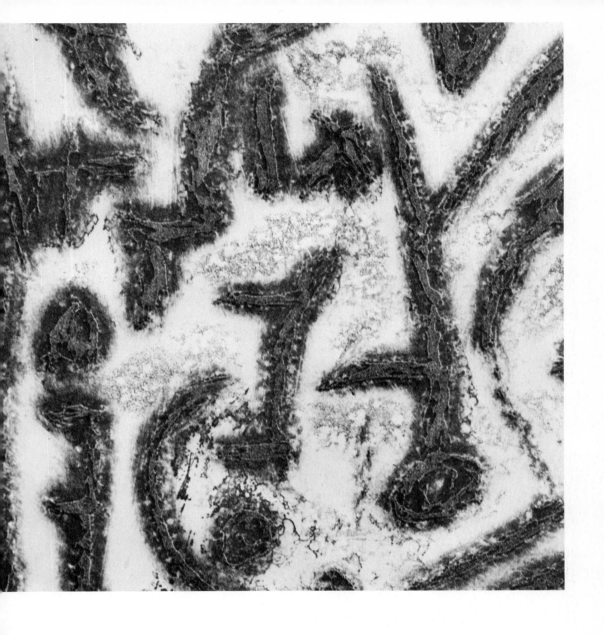

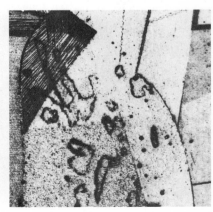

INTAGLIO PRINTING IN COLOR

The same procedures are followed in printing an intaglio plate in color as for an intaglio plate in black and white. The differences, and there are many, stem primarily from areas relating to the properties of color inks used individually and in combination. The color print in intaglio presents a real challenge even to the accomplished print-maker; no one has exhausted the range of possibilities in the medium. There is room for all to work in the field, to expand its horizons, and especially, to attempt color intaglio prints employing limited palettes of color.

Single Plate Printing in Color.

(1) As a point of departure for your first experiment in color intaglio printing, select an already worked plate upon which you have imposed a variety of technical approaches: etching, drypoint, aquatint, engraving, soft ground, etc. The greater the mosaic of techniques upon the plate, the more readily will you "see" and understand how color "works" in the different mediums in relation to your own handling of them.

Now, select a color etching ink or oil paint. Ink, wipe, and print the plate in the same way you print from black and white intaglio plates. You may stop at this point, if you so desire, and pull an edition of single color prints.

On the other hand, for those who wish to explore further the color printing aspects of the problem, place the print back in your damp box or water filled tray. Remove any trace of the previous color printed from the plate with a soft, clean cloth. Using a hard roller, ink the *surface* of your plate (as you would ink a relief block) with a different color.

Remove the one-color print from the damp box or water tray, place it between two clean, dry blotters to take off surface moisture, and place the relief-inked plate *face down* upon the already printed color image. A slight registration error should be sought to avoid "squashing" the lines. Now, holding the plate and paper firmly, turn them over and place them on the press bed with the plate underneath and the paper on top. Run the bed through the press slowly and evenly to obtain your first major experiment in color intaglio printing (see

Fig. III-13) . Examination of the following procedures should reveal one or more approaches that best answers your needs.

(2) The French method of color printing known as *à la poupée* consists of inking many colors in their separate areas with small pieces of felt, the fingers, and other devices and then printing them in a single run through the press. Although many visual atrocities have been committed with and by this particular technique, there is no technical reason for ignoring its possibilities.

(3) Still another variation may be obtained by inking the intagliate, printing it in one color or black, and then re-inking the intagliate with a different color and slightly off-register. The same might be done with the relief aspect of the same plate.

A masking technique may be employed to stop out all of the surface area except for particular forms. Stencil paper may be used to stop out the surface of the plate except where it is cut. Separate stencils for each color may be cut and printed individually to obtain precise edges not otherwise achieved.

Combinations of any of these methods of single plate printing may be used at the discretion of the printmaker.

Intaglio and Relief Color Printing from One Plate.

An intaglio design may be inked in the normal manner with black ink and the surface wiped especially clean. Color may be applied on the surface of the plate in the following ways:

(1) Stencils (one or more) may be cut and color litho ink rolled on the plate through the cut stencil with a gelatin brayer. If the color film is kept thin enough, it is possible to lay on more than one color side by side and in overlays. Print simultaneously (see Fig. III-16) .

(2) Oil paint may be brushed thinly in particular textured areas or sections of the surface. The black and white and the color are printed in one run through the press.

(3) On an aquatint or textured plate that is bitten *very deeply,* it is possible to scrub oil based crayon of many colors into the deeply bitten areas, and roll with a hard roller or a colored surface ink. Heat the plate just to the point where the wax melts and print on dry, soft paper. This technique was developed by Milton Goldstein, a student of Harry Sternberg (see Fig. III-59) .

(4) After an intaglio design has been inked in black or a colored

Fig. III-59. Milton Goldstein: "Landscape"

ink, it is possible to roll a colored ink into the deeply etched portions of the plate with a soft roller. Clean the surface again, and roll that surface with another colored ink and a hard roller. This is a variation of one of Boris Margo's techniques in his "cellocut" (see Figs. III-60 and III-61) .

(5) In the manner of the offset lithographic process, one can work from *any* inked-up printable surface onto a composition roller or half-drum (not inked) and transfer the same to the surface of a copper plate. This allows for great brilliancy of color, and has been used by Hayter and others.

Intaglio Color Printing from Two or More Plates.

The primary problem in working from two or more plates for color printing concerns the registration difficulty usually encountered. Registration for color work may be effected in any one of the following ways:

(1) The most primitive method, yet most simple, is achieved by working with plates of equal dimensions. After printing one color from the first plate, the second plate is inked with its color. Place the *print* with the first color face up on a flat, smooth surface. Take the second inked-up plate and place it squarely face down upon the print. Now, with some practice, you can acquire the knack of holding plate and paper firmly in place as you turn them upside down, place them on the press bed and print them. Some of my students have allowed them to go through the press with the plate on top and the paper on bottom. The third plate is registered by eye in the same manner, and

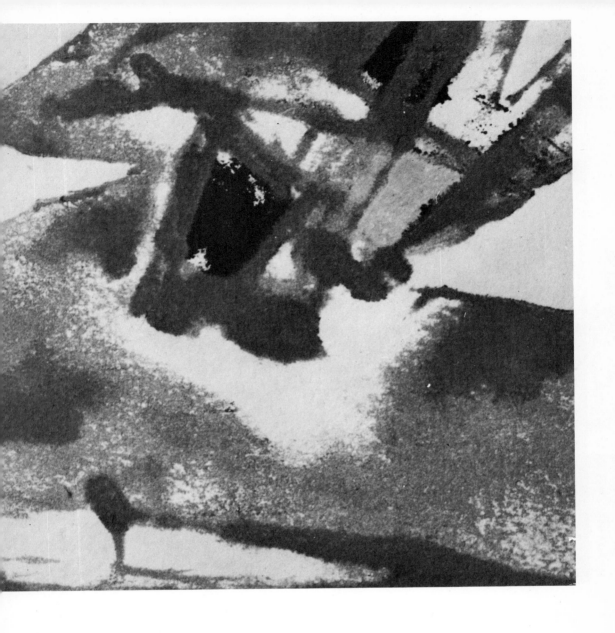

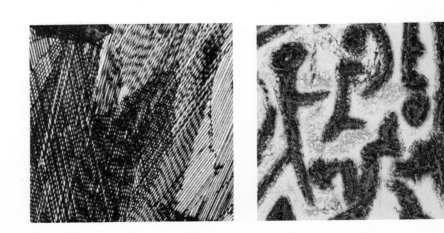

From Meteorites   23/200   cellocut   Boris Margo

should go through the press in the normal fashion—that is, with the plate on the bottom and the paper on the top—especially if it is the deepest etched. Lasansky uses a similar approach save that he employs a blanket *under* the plate when it is printed upside down the second time. Obviously, this will cause your plate to curl; since it is easily straightened when run through the press (this time face up, and without the blanket underneath), the method is quite acceptable.

(2) Another method of registration commonly used consists in drilling two tiny holes in the master plate at opposite ends from each other, then offsetting a print of the master plate *and* the holes onto each of the other color plates to be used. This is so like the method used in woodcut that the reader is asked to refer to page 95 for a more detailed explanation.

Without spelling out other contributions to the problem of registration, the author is certain that the new printmaker will evolve his own way in solving his individual problems. For those interested in reading of other approaches, the reader is referred to Hayter's excellent work.*

WORKSHOP SOLUTIONS TO INTAGLIO PRINTING PROBLEMS

The Printing Blankets Look and Feel Stiff.

Problem: Sizing from the printing paper has permeated the felt and dried hard.

Solution: Wash the blankets with soap and lukewarm water, and hang to dry; avoid stretching.

The Print Wrinkles when Pulled through the Press.

Problem: Blankets may be wet or stiff or wrinkled or stretched; printing paper may be unevenly damped; the paper may be wrong for this use.

Solution: Change the blankets; check the printing paper to make certain the edges are not dry; try other papers.

* Stanley William Hayter, *New Ways of Gravure* (New York: Pantheon, 1949).

Lines on the Print Have Smeared or Spread.

Problem: Pressure of the press too great; ink contains too much plate oil.

Solution: Reduce press pressure; add pigment to your ink, and regrind it thoroughly.

Print Surface Is Shiny.

Problem: Press pressure is too great; plate may be too hot; blankets may be wet or stiff with size.

Solution: Reduce press pressure; cool the plate; change the blankets.

Some of the Lines Did Not Print, or Did Not Print Well.

Problem: Ink may be too dry, gritty, or too stiff; press may have too little pressure; plate may not be level and may need a makeready; paper may be too wet or too dry; foreign substances (e.g. whiting, stop-out) may reside in the intagliate; careless inking of the plate.

Solution: Mix a fresh batch of ink adding more plate oil than before; check press pressure; test level of plate and correct, if necessary, with a makeready (see below); correct the condition of the paper; clean the intagliate thoroughly, using the proper solvent; observe and follow the wiping procedure recommended on page 137.

One Part of a Large Plate (Usually the Center) Refuses to Print.

Problem: The plate is not level.

Solution: Glue a makeready (enough thicknesses of paper to correct the deficiency) to the back of the plate, under the troublesome area, and proceed with your work of printing.

In Printing from a Drypoint Plate, the Ink Quality Seems Poor.

Problem: The ink is too thin.

Solution: Add more pigment to the ink and/or a heavier varnish.

In Printing from a Plate Worked with the Burin, the Ink Quality Seems Poor.

Problem: The ink is too stiff.
Solution: Use an ink which contains some raw linseed oil and/or add more plate oil to your ink.

Areas Intended as Relief Whites Are Printing as Darks, or Carry Dark Edges.

Problem: Assuming the fault is not in the bitten work or burin line in the plate, ink was wiped unintentionally into these areas.
Solution: Use a cotton swab or a Q-tip to clean the line or area thoroughly before placing the inked plate on the press bed.

A Dense Film Covers the Print; It Lacks Sharp Definition.

Problem: This is primarily a matter of wiping. Sometimes it reflects a rag wipe—if too oily a rag was employed.
Solution: Try a final hand wipe before printing from your plate. Also you may, if you desire little or no film in background areas, rub whiting on the heel of your palm before wiping. Be sure to remove excess whiting from your hand before wiping.

Print Lacks a Film of Ink, the Ink Quality Is Poor.

Problem: Probably due to too much whiting used on the hand during the final wipe; ink too stiff; too many wiping strokes employed.
Solution: Use less whiting; add light plate oil to your ink; wipe when the plate still seems hot to your hands, and employ a minimum number of strokes in making the final hand wipe.

One Side of Your Print Shows a Double Impression.

Problem: Occurs sometimes to those printmakers who prefer to run all plates under the roller twice. A slight inequality in press pressure is enough to make a plate twist and double print on one side only.

Solution: Check roller pressure on both sides and adjust accordingly; perhaps the plate itself is buckled.

Print Tears or Sticks to Plate after Printing.

Problem: Removal is too rapid or abrupt; ink too tacky.

Solution: Peel print from one corner of the plate slowly; reheat the plate, or add more plate oil to the ink.

Your Prints Do Not Dry Flat.

Problem: Damp paper is stretched considerably in the printing of an intaglio plate. Unless you take the necessary steps to ensure flattening of your prints after they are printed, you can be certain they will buckle as they dry.

Solution: Rewet the prints in a tray full of clean water, and then with butcher tape secure them by their outer edges to a large piece of three-quarter inch plywood. When dry, they will have stretched flat.

Your Plate Curls when Pulled through the Press.

Problem: This is inevitable when the plate is placed improperly on the bed of the press.

Solution: Place the plate squarely in the middle of the press bed making certain its longest side is parallel with the axis of the press roller.

The Print Is Cut at the Plate Mark.

Problem: Both printing paper and blankets may be cut if the plate has not been beveled prior to printing.

Solution: File and polish a bevel on all four sides of your plate; do not use a cut blanket again.

You Have No Press and Wish to Proof Your Plate, or You Simply Desire to Make a Plaster Print.

Problem: How to make a plaster print.

Solution: Ink your plate in black ink or color as for normal press printing, save that the ink should be thinned somewhat. Lay your plate face up on a clean glass slab. Make a wooden frame (or use clay or cardboard) at least three-quarters of an inch high, whose inside dimensions equal the mat size you would normally employ for displaying that print. Secure the frame to the glass by weights, tape, clay, etc. Mix plaster of Paris, fine dental plaster, or a convenient substitute to a creamy consistency, and just before it starts to set pour and spread it evenly into the frame or mold. A few sharp blows from your hand on the work surface should break any stubborn bubbles in the plaster. The plaster print may be reinforced with burlap or similar material; a twisted wire hook may be pushed into the plaster before it finally sets, or screw eyes may be twisted into the wooden frame to allow for hanging. Finally, when the plaster has set, turn the frame over. Remove the plate carefully by inserting a knife blade at a likely point—and there you have your plaster print. Many printmakers further work this framed plaster print by additional carving, paint, etc.

BIBLIOGRAPHY: THE INTAGLIO PRINT

Barry, John J., *How to Make Etchings*. New York: Bridgman Publishers, 1929, 64 pp.

Bishop, Thomas, *The Etcher's Guide*. Philadelphia: Janentzky and Co., 1879. 22 pp.

Buckland-Wright, John, *Etching and Engraving. Techniques and the Modern Trend*. London: The Studio Publications, 1953. 240 pp.

Hamerton, Philip G., *Etching and Etchers*. Boston: Roberts Bros., 1878. 459 pp.

Hamerton, Philip G., *The Graphic Arts*. Boston: Roberts Bros., 1882. 508 pp.

Hayter, Stanley W., *New Ways of Gravure*. New York: Pantheon, 1949. 274 pp.

Holman, Louis A., *The Graphic Processes*. Boston: C. E. Goodspeed and Co., 1926. 54 l.

Lalanne, Maxime, *Treatise on Etching*. Translated from 2nd French ed. by S. R. Koehler. Boston: Estes and Lauriat, 1885. 79 pp.

Lumsden, Ernest S., *The Art of Etching*. Philadelphia: J. B. Lippincott Co., 1925. 376 pp.

Morrow, B. F., *The Art of Aquatint*. New York: G. P. Putnam's Sons, 1935. 140 pp.

Pennell, Joseph, *The Graphic Arts*. Chicago: University of Chicago Press, 1921. 315 pp.

Plowman, George T., *Etching and Other Graphic Arts*. New York: J. Lane Co., 1914. 154 pp.

Prideaux, Sarah T., *Aquatint Engraving*. London: Duckworth and Co., 1909. 434 pp.

Pyle, Clifford, *Etching Principles and Methods*. New York: Harper and Bros., 1941. 180 pp.

Reed, Earl H., *Etching, A Practical Treatise*. New York: G. P. Putnam's Sons, 1914. 148 pp.

Silsby, Wilson, *Etching Methods and Materials*. New York: Dodd, Mead, and Co., 1943. 114 pp.

Sternberg, Harry, *Modern Methods and Materials of Etching*. New York: McGraw-Hill Book Co., 1949. 146 pp.

Torrey, Frederic C., *The Art of Etching*. Berkeley: University of California Press, 1923. 18 pp.

West, Levon, *Making an Etching*. London: The Studio Ltd., 1932 79 pp.

"The true discoverer is not the man who first chances to stumble upon anything, but the man who finds what he has sought."
JACOB BURCKHARDT: *The Civilization of the Renaissance in Italy.*

IV

The Stencil Process:
Serigraphy

THE DEVELOPMENT and extension of serigraphy as a fine arts medium for the printmaker grew out of the economic crisis in the America of the 1930's and the great stimulus of the WPA Federal Arts Project. About two years after the project was initiated, a separate silk screen unit of the New York City WPA Art Project was set up with Anthony Velonis as its head; and, less than two years after that, Guy Maccoy held the first one-man show of silk screen stencil prints at the Contemporary Arts Gallery in the same city. Elizabeth McCausland, in reviewing several group shows of serigraphs, caught the fervor of the times with these words:

> There is an exciting historical portent in the speed with which the silk screen color print has captured the fancy of contemporary graphic artists. It is as exciting as if in 1800, two years after Alois Senefelder had discovered lithography, the French Academy—amid the throes of Napoleonic politics—had held a large group exhibition of lithographs. Or as if in 1842, two years after Daguerre's invention had been intro-

duced into the United States, a large exhibition of daguerreotypes had been held at the non-existent Metropolitan Museum of Art.*

Many men working individually and in concert throughout our vast country were almost simultaneously responsible for the burgeoning of the silk screen stencil print—christened "serigraphy" by Carl Zigrosser, eminent Curator of Prints at the Philadelphia Museum of Art. Especial credit should be granted the pioneering technical and esthetic achievements of Anthony Velonis. Guy Maccoy, Hyman Warsager, Edward Landon, Elizabeth Olds, Harry Gottlieb, Mervin Jules, Ruth Gikow, and Harry Sternberg are but a few of the early leaders in the medium.

This versatile process offers such challenging color possibilities and such richly satisfying optical effects that many printmakers, in a short-sighted view of the field, tend to be seduced into overstatement; they tend to compete with paintings through their use of an extravagant number of screens. On the other hand, an extravagant amount of time is required to produce a serigraph that fulfills its pictorial idea with a *minimum of means*. Fortunately, there are practitioners of the medium whose sensitivity towards the silk screen color print is such as to merit acclaim. At this juncture in the history of printmaking, serigraphy is on the march. Despite the highly vocal minority that succeeds in barring this medium from certain exhibitions of prints because no "press" is employed in making an edition, the serigraph holds its own on a wall next to the etching, engraving, lithograph, wood engraving, and woodcut. It grows in stature year by year, and is likely to stay.

Basically, the serigraph is a stencil process. In this particular case, the stencil is affixed to a piece of silk stretched tightly across a wooden frame. The physical structure of silk is such as to allow paint to be forced or "squeegeed" through its warp and woof. Areas not to be printed are "blocked out" on the silk screen itself—that is, the pores of the silk are closed wherever desired, thus preventing paint from penetrating at those points. If a sheet of paper is placed underneath such a silk screen stencil before paint is forced through the mesh, the paint will be deposited upon the paper. For each color to be employed in securing the final print, a separate stencil is required. The proper combination of "block-out" and paint permits the printmaker the

* Elizabeth McCausland, "Silk Screen Color Prints," *Parnassus* (March, 1940).

use of various color mediums—from dyes and oil colors to lacquers, enamels, poster paints, and other synthetic products.

Planning a Serigraph.

The technical considerations in serigraphy, though they are many, are simple enough to be mastered in short order. Consequently, the printmaker can and should concentrate upon his particular pictorial image. Should he allow it to evolve screen by screen without too much control at first? Does he feel more secure working from a carefully rendered image in color? Is it necessary to observe a certain order in printing the individual colors? Must transparent colors follow opaque or semi-opaque pigments? Does the answer to all of these questions emerge from the experience of the printmaker in interaction with a specific visual idea? Let us pursue these questions further:

On the basis of much observation, there appears to be a body of serigraphers who prefer to find their particular print *in the process* of making a serigraph. That is, without a well-defined visual idea in mind, they proceed to invent and superimpose one screen upon another with seeming disregard for the final effect. At some point within this process, control is exercised and a whole is welded together from these seemingly unrelated parts.

When this approach yields a successful print (speaking in terms of the individual artist's goals), it is usually because the *method* of working was in accord with the total experience of the artist. The approach is not employed for itself alone; there are many occasions in which this evolving approach leads to disaster because insufficient control was exercised, or because it was too arbitrary a way of working for a particular individual.

More commonly, an artist will work out a color sketch prior to attempting to make a serigraph. Usually he will enlarge the sketch to the maximum printing format of his screens. This step produces a master sketch which can be placed beneath the silk screen for simple tracing. Let us re-examine this aspect of the procedure: We have just completed a sketch in color of an image which we regard as significant (else why the need to multiply this image many times?). Now, what is the best way, for ourselves, of "atomizing" our sketch into many parts so that we can put it together in a different medium (the serigraph) to form a new whole, somewhat similar to our sketch, but "different"?

The obvious answer, though not necessarily the best, is to have a plan so complete in color that one merely traces area for area, line for line, texture for texture, and so forth *from* the sketch *to* the screen on successive stencils. On the other hand, a device which allowed the sketch to be broken down into its component parts and still permitted variations upon each part *before* the whole was crystallized in an edition would, it seems, be most helpful to many artists. This may easily be done by making individual color separations from the master sketch on cellulose acetate, or its equivalent, with transparent color inks, dyes, or paints. Now, one can examine the individual parts in their approximate colors as well as the total effect of the whole color ensemble *before* the actual printing is accomplished. Are there any changes which suggest themselves on any one or more of the individual color runs? Is the total image improved or not by the subtraction or addition of one or more of the color separations? With all of the separations superimposed and held up to the light together, are you satisfied with what you see? If not, how should you make the necessary changes and alterations to improve the total image? Is this approach more flexible than the first, or is it merely an extension introducing still another material which takes the whole problem still farther away from the thing that is serigraphy?

MATERIALS, TOOLS, AND EQUIPMENT

Making a Printing Frame.

For those who prefer to engage in some elementary carpentry work rather than buy a readymade frame, these are the materials required: silk, a good grade of seasoned lumber 2″ by 2″ by 12′, 4 angle irons, a roll of brown wrapping tape, a good hand-stapling machine, clear synthetic enamel or acetate dope, and a brush.

1. THE SILK. Although there are many other materials which also substitute for silk (Swiss bolting cloth, organdie, bronze wire cloth, nylon, taffeta, etc.), most printmakers still prefer the original material made for serigraphy. Silk is sold in standard widths ranging from 40 inches to 60 inches; there is a standard weight (x) and a double, extra heavy weight (xx). It is available in coarse (6x or 6xx) to very fine weaves (17x or 17xx to 20x or 20xx). The number of the silk or bolting cloth refers to the number of threads per square inch. For

average use, 12xx is highly recommended. In purchasing your silk, be certain to buy enough to cover the *outside* dimensions of your printing frame.

As an example (Fig. IV-1), we have selected a frame which would allow the printing of a 20″ by 30″ picture. The outside dimensions of the wooden printing frame measure 30 by 40 inches. One yard of 40″ wide 12xx silk will adequately meet our needs. While smaller work may be done on a large screen, the reverse is, of course, impossible.

2. THE FRAME. The frame should be hinged to a baseboard larger in area than itself. This baseboard may be a drawing table, board, piece of marine plywood, etc., so long as it is level and smooth. The hinges should contain a pin that allows being withdrawn in removing one screen and replacing another. These are called loose-pin hinges (see Figs. IV-7 and IV-8).

If more than one frame is used, so order the hinges that all the frames will fit the same baseboard. This involves some careful planning that will save much time later on.

Fig. IV-1. Diagram of a printing frame for serigraphy.

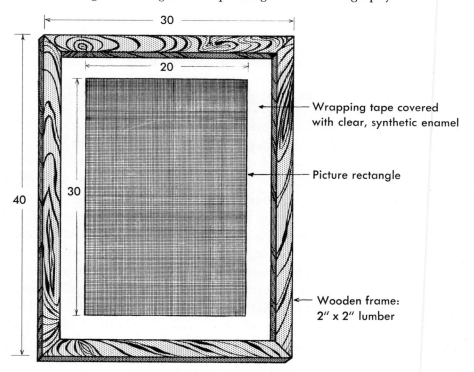

Wrapping tape covered with clear, synthetic enamel

Picture rectangle

Wooden frame: 2″ x 2″ lumber

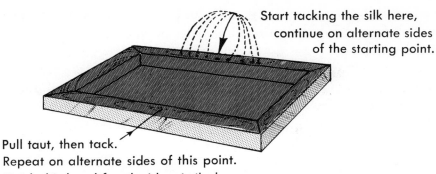

Start tacking the silk here,
continue on alternate sides
of the starting point.

Pull taut, then tack.
Repeat on alternate sides of this point.
Finish third and fourth sides similarly.

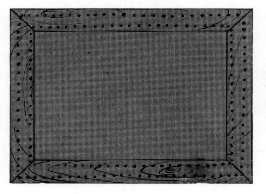

At this stage,
the stretched frame
should look like this.

Fig. IV-2. Stretching the silk.

Stretching the Silk.

Cut the silk slightly larger than the frame to allow for tacking it down. Line up the warp and woof of the fabric so that it runs parallel to the frame, and will thus insure proper stretching. Our purpose now is to stretch the silk as tightly as possible without injuring it. No matter what type of frame we use, or whether we staple or tack it down, the silk should be stretched as a painter stretches his canvas.

Start tacking or stapling the silk from the middle of one of the longer sides of the frame, according to Figure IV-2. Keep the fabric parallel to the frame as you staple alternately on both sides of the starting point. You now have one side completely tacked down. Now, stretch the silk taut from the center of the side opposite your original starting point, and tack it down. Keep stretching and tacking on alternate sides of the second starting point. Do the same for the third and fourth shorter sides of the frame.

There are other methods for stretching silk across the frame. However, let us examine the one employed with the grooved sides. Substituting the fibre rope for tacks, the process is precisely the same. When the rope holds the silk fast on all four sides of the frame, the silk may be made even tighter by tapping a wooden wedge into the grooves with a hammer.

Complete the frame by applying butcher's tape over the staples or tacks holding the silk in place. Turn the frame over; cut four more pieces of tape equivalent to the four inside dimensions of the frame. Fold each piece in half, gummed side out. Apply these strips to the inside of the frame so that half of each strip sits on the wood while the other half covers the silk. Brush a coating of shellac or acetate dope over the tape to further seal the juncture between the wood and the silk. Done carefully, this eliminates paint from seeping through the frame to spoil the print. Further, its purpose is to keep paint from gathering and hardening under the frame and eventually cutting the silk at this juncture. Be wary of allowing droplets of shellac or dope to drop or spatter on the screen itself. Errors of this sort may be rectified *immediately* by applying the proper solvent to the area.

The sizing may be removed from the silk by careful washing with a detergent after it is stretched upon the frame. Remember that the silk should be as taut as the skin across a drum.

The Squeegee.

As the burin is to engraving and the lithographic roller is to the planographic printing process, so the squeegee relates to the problem of fine prints in serigraphy. As with all tools in the graphic arts, this one must be kept in proper working order to function effectively. It is the instrument by which paint is forced through the screen to contact the printing paper; consequently, it must have no nicks, must be perfectly level and sharp at all times. The rubber blade should be sharpened on fine sandpaper or emery cloth from time to time, and should be examined carefully *before* each new color application for defects.

It is a simple tool containing a rubber blade inserted in a wooden handle. Obviously, one should purchase a squeegee which can be manipulated within the *inside* dimensions of the printing frame.

Fig. IV-3. Sealing paper tape on the frame.

For different effects, it is possible to use squeegees with soft, medium, or hard rubber blades. It would be advisable to use the medium rubber blade when attempting your first project in this medium.

MAKING A SERIGRAPH

Now let us follow the step-by-step procedure in the making of a serigraph, employing direct, simple, foolproof means to accomplish our purpose. We will assume our silk screen frame is already constructed.

Sealing the Frame.

We have just taped the stapled edges on the back side and sealed the tape against disintegration by coating it with shellac, clear synthetic enamel, or, as in this instance, with acetate dope. Figure IV-3 shows the sealing of the inner sides of the frame. The protective seal not only covers the brown wrapping tape, but overlaps onto the silk itself, making certain that pigment will not penetrate the juncture and spoil the prints in process.

15

KEY TO DETAILS

1. Lithograph
2. Mixed medium (Intaglio)
3. Aquatint
4. Woodcut
5. Lift ground
6. Drypoint
7. Wood engraving
8. Soft ground
9. Cellocut
10. Linoleum cut
11. Engraving
12. Deep etch and relief
13. Etching
14. Mezzotint
15. Serigraph

13

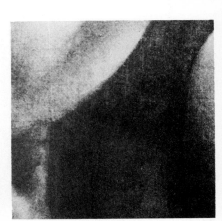

14

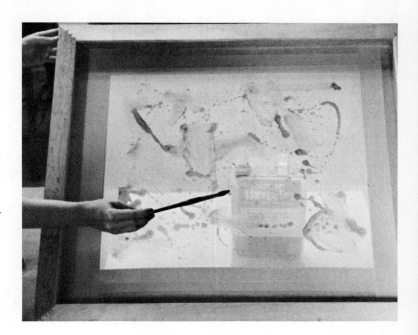

Fig. IV-6. Applying water-soluble resist to the screen.

Designing the Stencil.

With the hope of stimulating readers to work freely within the medium of serigraphy, the author selected to show this most direct, spontaneous approach (Fig. IV-6). Use a mixture of equal parts of LePage's glue and water, or, as in this instance, a commercial water soluble substance called WaterSol to brush, spatter, dab, and dot the silk with a stick, brush, syringe, hypodermic needle, etc. In a few minutes the WaterSol becomes a dry, tough, elastic, nonshrinking block-out that allows working the screen. WaterSol is easily removed in *cold* water; *hot* water makes it *insoluble*. There should be no attempt, at this point, to exercise control of any sort; deliberately plan to start organizing your serigraph *after* this and one or two other spontaneously-made screens have been printed in succession, in different hues upon the trial printing paper.

Providing for Registration.

How can we be sure our second screen, and all the others that follow, falls accurately in place over our previous runs? This is the problem of registration—one that has many solutions. Figure IV-7 dem-

Fig. IV-7 (left). One method of registration.

Fig. IV-8 (below). Locking the frame to the baseboard.

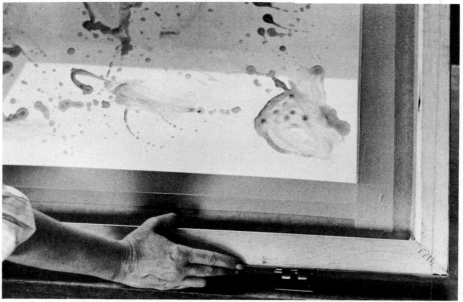

onstrates one answer. Plastic registration guides or tabs have been affixed with tape to the tabletop seen in the photograph to make certain the printing paper will be lined up accurately. These inexpensive, plastic tabs are more accurate than their paper or tape equivalents. Our printing paper is made to slide home against the two tabs on the bottom of the photograph, then against the tab on the right, thus insuring registration.

Fig. IV-9. Preparing the paint.

Locking the Frame.

Since we cannot see how our printing frame is secured to the baseboard or tabletop, let us turn to Figure IV-8. As is evident, the frame is secured by means of a removable pin-hinge. Here, we are locking the hinges on the frame to their already secured mates on the tabletop. The pins are inserted when both parts of each hinge mesh.

Mixing the Paint.

In Figure IV-9 we are mixing paint to the consistency of heavy cream. The paint, in this instance, is a combination of transparent base with Wornowink. The amount of transparent base used with your color is not overly critical; add as much base, up to 50 percent, as is desired. The manufacturer of Wornowink suggests 4 parts of clear base to 1 part color plus the necessary mineral spirits. (Our differences are quite obvious.) It is not necessary to use only the mediums manufactured especially for serigraphy. Artist's oil colors, ignoring cost, are wonderfully adaptable, especially for transparent effects. How much paint should be mixed? The size of your print will determine the amount of color to be used. Roughly, a quart of paint is adequate for an edition of fifty normal-sized prints (meaning you will pull about sixty or more).

Pulling and Drying the Print.

With our batch of paint mixed, and the screen dry, add a generous line of paint at one end of the frame, and squeegee it across to the other end. Figure IV-10 shows the operation clearly.

Raise the screen and remove the print (Fig. IV-11). Now, before we go ahead and pull the rest of our edition—in this particular stage —we have to face the problem of drying the prints. How and where do you find enough space in which to dry fifty or sixty wet prints? One answer to the problem lies in stringing lines of wooden clothespins across your workroom at a convenient height. Hanging two wet prints back-to-back from one clothespin allows you to dry numbers of them in a comparatively small space. For those who have access to the drying racks used commercially, this simple expedient may seem overly primitive. But, each printmaker, in the privacy of his studio, seems to work out his own solutions to these mechanical problems in short order.

When this color dries, the print is ready for the next screen, and the next. (With Wornowink your prints are air-dry in under 30 minutes.) The same procedure, more or less, is carried on for each additional screen until the serigraph is complete.

Cleaning the Screen.

When the last print in a given run is squeegeed, use a number of cardboard rectangles (2″ by 4″) to remove most of the paint from the frame.

Place a thick layer of newspapers on a work surface and lay your screen on top of them. Using a large rag saturated with mineral spirits or the equivalent, wash out the screen thoroughly on both sides. Keep removing the saturated newspapers under the screen from time to time to allow for a more efficient clean-up. When the paint appears to have been removed, wipe the screen dry on both sides with a clean, dry, lint-free rag. The screen may be stored away if you wish to save the stencil for future runs.

If you own but *one* silk screen frame, and have to use the same frame again and again for each separate run, the removal of a water soluble stencil is accomplished as follows:

To remove a WaterSol or glue stencil, soak your screen in a tray

Fig. IV-10 (above). Squeegeeing paint across the screen.

Fig. IV-11 (below). The print at its first stage of development.

of *cold* water, or run water from a hose upon it as your hands gently massage the silk. These water soluble stencils come off the silk quite easily and quickly.

This spontaneous, technically simple approach merely serves to act as the prologue to other approaches to serigraphy. Try them all to discover which best suits your specific visual needs.

OTHER APPROACHES TO SERIGRAPHY

Tusche-resist Method.

This is the most autographic method of all of the approaches to the silk screen, and the one, therefore, in highest repute among serigraphers. It is not an involved affair; it can be learned in an afternoon; yet, it can produce as complex a color image as one would desire. At the same time, since complexity never was a criterion for art, the medium used by an artist sensitive to these particular materials is only beginning to assert itself.

The principle involved in the tusche method is similar in many ways to that of the lift ground in the intaglio process. The image is painted on the screen with tusche (grease suspended in a liquid) and a brush and allowed to dry. A half-glue and half-water mixture is scraped across the entire screen covering the drawing. When this glue mixture is dry, it is washed with a solvent that affects only the tusche drawing and not the glue. This leaves the silk *open* wherever you have drawn with tusche; the glue, resting on the undrawn areas, acts as a stencil or resist when paint is forced through the silk with a squeegee.

Stop-out Method.

This is the method illustrated in Figures IV-6 through IV-11. Those printmakers with experience in the intaglio field will find this approach quite familiar. A resist or stop-out is painted directly upon the silk screen to all of the areas that do not require color. When dry, the paint is placed at one end of the screen and squeegeed across to the other side. This simple approach offers many possibilities both in terms of the variety of materials one can employ and the diversity of final results. Also, this approach permits the print to grow organically without complex mechanical interference.

If the resist used is glue and water, oil paint may be screened through the silk. Check the use of other materials by referring to the chart that follows:

Resist or Stencil on Screen	Paint or Ink Suggested
Glue	Oil base, lacquers, plastic inks
Lacquer filler	Oil base, water base, enamels, dyes
Lacquer film stencil	Oil base
Paper stencil	Oil base
Plastic-backed water soluble film	Synthetic lacquers, vinyl lacquers
Photographic stencil	Lacquer, oils, any water-free paint
Shellac	Water base, lacquer

Paper Stencils.

Without resorting to more complex procedures, you may affix torn or cut paper to the bottom of the silk screen and run off more than is normally pulled in an edition. The stencil can be adhered by the silk screen paint itself as the squeegee is drawn across the silk, provided it has been located properly *under* the screen beforehand.

Glue-Shellac Method.

Mix equal parts of glue and water to which a few drops of glycerine are added. Prop up the screen so that the silk is raised above your working surface and does not touch any other surface.

Using a leveled scrap of mat board or cardboard, squeegee the glue mixture over the silk on the inside of the frame. Cover the screen with the glue mixture in two or more directions. Let the glue dry.

Now, check the silk carefully to make certain there are no unfilled pores or pinholes through which you can see light. If you find any such places, touch them with a soft brush dipped in the glue mixture; if there are many pinholes, reduce the consistency of the glue mixture by adding more water to it, and add another coat. When the screen is totally sized with glue, and is dry, we may proceed to the next step.

Using lacquer or shellac (most serigraphers select black), brush out all the negative areas—those you do *not* wish to print. Do not cut the lacquer or shellac too thin for this purpose, as they will be the resist. Hold the screen up to the light when the resist is dry, and check once more for pinholes. Correct accordingly.

Place the screen once more in a horizontal position raised slightly off your work table. Using a soft, clean rag and a pan of water, gently work over the inside of the screen. Do not allow the water to saturate the screen all at once, but slowly—by wiping and picking up excess water with the rag—remove the glue from the open areas. You will find this process to be one wherein you start with a water-charged rag, wipe, wring out the rag to remove the excess water, and repeat again and again until the open glue areas are all dissolved. Finish wiping the screen with a dry rag.

Using the Lacquer Stencil Film.

For meticulously precise edges and other geometric approaches, it is recommended that one become familiar with the lacquer stencil film. This film, known in the trade as nufilm, profilm, etc., is a laminated stencil composed of a colored lacquer film and a sheet of glassine paper. The stencil (the lacquer film) must be cut without penetrating the glassine paper (the backing), because the backing holds the isolated areas (e.g., the center of the letter "O") in place until you transfer the film to the silk screen.

Be certain the cutting knife you use is especially sharp; a short practice period will allow you to "feel" the proper cutting depth, and keep you from going through the glassine backing.

With the stencil cut and the printing portions removed from their backing (all except the islands), the problem is to affix the stencil to the silk screen. Place the stencil under the silk screen so that the two are in firm contact. Using film-adhering liquid on a small, clean rag, rub firmly and dry immediately with a rag held in the other hand. Repeat this wet and dry rubbing procedure until the stencil is firmly adhered to the silk screen. By cutting a slit or two through the backing of any large area to be printed you will have a trouble-free join.

A small electric fan will hasten the drying and allow you, then, to peel the backing from the stencil. If, on removing the backing, the stencil seems to be lifting—stop, and repeat the adhering procedure again. Block out the open silk between the edges of the stencil and the frame by taping the areas, applying paper, or stopping out with lacquer screen filler.

From this point on, you may go ahead with the printing.

Imitation Shellac Method.

In this approach to the silk screen, the image is drawn on the silk with glue—that is, the positive is brushed on the clean, bare silk. This is similar to the tusche-resist method. It may be helpful to add a coloring agent to the glue to allow you to see the image more clearly. Allow the glue to dry.

Prop up the screen as for many of the other approaches, and squeegee the imitation shellac over the screen in two or more directions. When this is dry and free from pinholes, apply water to both sides of the screen and rub thoroughly with a soft rag. The water soluble glue will begin to swell underneath the imitation shellac, and will soon give way, leaving the silk open in the desired areas. Now, you are ready to print.

This method is useful for opaque watercolor (tempera), but may not be used with normal screen process paints. The screen process paints, because of the varnishes within them, would "melt" the imitation shellac stencil.

When the run is completed, the imitation shellac stencil may be removed from the screen with denatured alcohol.

Using Photographic Stencils.

The use of photographic stencils, though frowned upon by some "purists" in the medium, may occasionally be the printmaker's only solution to his problem. This may be especially true in cases where very fine lettering is needed in conjunction with the pictorial idea. Further, the photographic method holds great promise in achieving textural effects and gradated color qualities not possible in any of the other techniques. A photographic stencil may be employed alone or in combination with any of the aforementioned approaches to stencil making. Obviously, it is difficult, if not impossible, to suggest all of the reasons for the employment of the photographic stencil.

Photographic stencils may be made in many ways; manufacturers supply detailed instructions for use of their individual products; there are direct photo stencils, indirect photo stencils, the carbon tissue method, and others. All, however, operate on the principle of light-hardened gelatin. Let us clarify this in some detail, using the indirect method as an example:

Given a source of light, a photographic positive, and a light-sensitive gelatin film, in this order, we may proceed.

Let us assume the photographic positive and the light-sensitive gelatin film (supported on a transparent backing) are locked together, emulsion sides facing each other, in a photographic vacuum printing frame. Exposure to light *hardens* all the gelatin areas under the *transparent* parts of the photographic positive, and leaves undisturbed (or *soft*) those areas under the *opaque* parts of the photographic positive.

Consequently, when the gelatin film is removed from the vacuum frame and "developed" or "etched" in hot water, the unhardened areas of the film wash out. This leaves the light-hardened sections of the film as a resist, providing you with a photographic stencil easily transferred to your silk screen. When the stencil is dry, after firm contact has been made with the silk, remove the backing of the photographic stencil and print in the usual way.

Now, if for the photographic positive we substitute our own design drawn with opaque ink on transparent acetate, or if we have a film positive made from one of our sketches, we can readily understand the possibilities and great potential inherent in the photographic screen stencil.

A GALLERY OF SERIGRAPHS

The serigraphs that follow are not intended to present all that has been accomplished in this medium, nor all that may be accomplished in the future; these are merely a selected group of prints that indicate divergent approaches currently practiced.

Richly pigmented, Byzantine-like in style. "This Beginning of Miracles" by Sister Mary Corita (Fig. IV-12) glows auralike on a

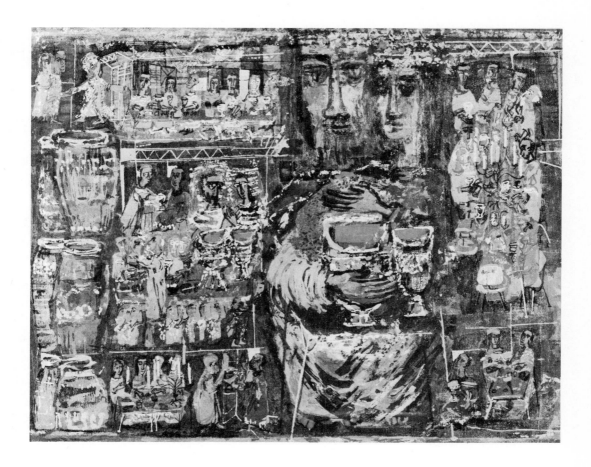

Fig. IV-12. Sister Mary Corita: "This Beginning of Miracles"

wall. Using the stop-out method illustrated in Figs. IV-6 through IV-11, Sister Corita builds up her complex images screen by screen to achieve her pictorial requirements. Contrast her many-faceted composition with the startling serigraph, "Northern Winter," by Edward Landon (Fig. IV-13). Landon seeks and finds his visual idea with a minimum of screens. His symbolism seems to possess the solidity of Stonehenge.

Guy Maccoy, one of the pioneers in the medium, brings a high degree of craftsmanship and the almost "traditional" tusche-resist approach to his "Melon and Apples" (Fig. IV-14). The flexibility of the tusche-resist way is quite apparent in Maccoy's dotted textures, bold, decorative line, and heavily pigmented areas on the apple forms. "Micromystic" (Fig. IV-15), by Robert W. Brown, offers a nonfigurative way of working that is rich in textural detail. The light lines which run through the serigraph were obtained by using such unorthodox tools as hypodermic needles and syringes filled with a stop-out solution. When these dried, paint was squeegeed across these nonprinting areas.

Hulda Robbins obtains a free, direct line in combination with thin washes of color in "Beacon" (Fig. IV-16). Effects such as this are obtained through the tusche-resist approach or the stop-out method (see page 216). Her simplified, seemingly spontaneous technique heightens the mood of the print. In contrast, "Hammerhead Blues" (Fig. IV-17) by James McConnell, suggests the complex, mathematical precision of "advanced jazz." His approach stems from the lacquer stencil film approach (see page 218).

Thin, painterly textures lying beneath a network of organiclike, heavy filaments appear in "Dark Wings" (Fig. IV-18) by Sylvia Wald. Experimentation in squeegee pressure, paint consistency, and speed in lifting the screen from the print may produce similar effects. The veteran serigrapher, Harry Shokler, displays his fine sense of craftsmanship in "Netmenders" (Fig. IV-19).

Phillip Lejeune in his "Hercule et Omphale" (Fig. IV-20) weds his figures to their shallow stage in a series of thin overlays of screened pigment. "New Series #2" (Fig. IV-21) by Harold Krisel achieves nonobjective purity in its meticulous geometry. Here again, we see complete control of the lacquer stencil film.

The highly decorative "Sunflower" (Fig. IV-22) by Glen Alps seems sedate and gentle in its straightforward technical approach when compared with the violently textured "Nocturne" (Fig. IV-23) by Henry Marks.

It should be apparent at this juncture that there is no single way to make a serigraph. The vision of each printmaker can "break through" any series of methods and techniques to create a personal statement.

Fig. IV-13 (above). Edward Landon: "Northern Winter"

Fig. IV-14 (below). Guy Maccoy: "Melon and Apples"

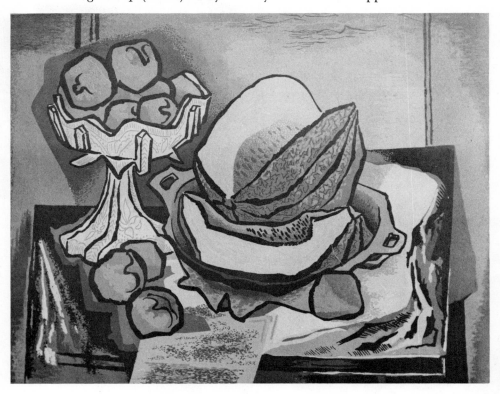

Fig. IV-15 (above). Robert W. Brown: "Micromystic"

Fig. IV-16 (right). Hulda Robbins: "Beacon"

Fig. IV-17 (below). James H. McConnell: "Hammerhead Blues"

Fig. IV-18 (opposite page). Sylvia Wald: "Dark Wings" (sideways)

Fig. IV-19 (above). Harry Shokler: "Netmenders"

Fig. IV-20 (left). Phillip Lejeune: "Hercule et Omphale"

Fig. IV-21 (opposite page). Harold Krisel: "New Series #2"

Fig. IV-22. Glen Alps: "Sunflower"

WORKSHOP SOLUTIONS TO SERIGRAPHIC PROBLEMS

You Can't Wash Out Your Tusche Drawing from the Screen.

Problem: The tusche applied was too thin or the glue mixture was too thick.

Solution: Instead of rags, try using a nail brush, toothbrush, or an equivalent tool. Do not scrub in an overly rough manner or you will damage the silk.

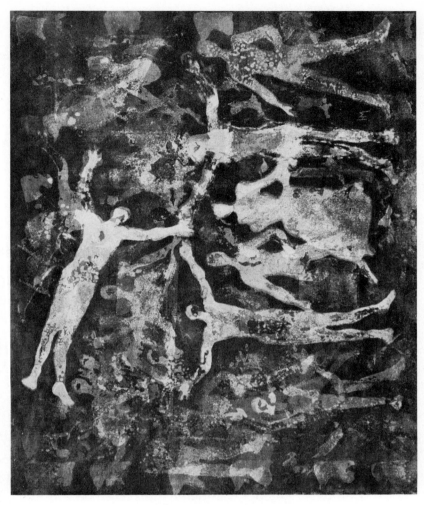

Fig. IV-23. Henry Mark: "Nocturne"

The Screen Clogs While You Are Printing.

Problem: The paint dried too rapidly, closing the pores of the silk.

Solution: Remove the screen and wash with a rag and solvent. Add mixing varnish or transparent base to your paint plus a few drops of Varnoline or mineral spirits.

Problem: Lint from printing paper or rags or tissues is responsible.

Solution: Run a still moist print under the screen. The lint will be picked off in that manner.

Registration of the Print Becomes Faulty.

Problem: Registration guides or tabs have gotten out of alignment.
Solution: Realign and test.

Problem: The hinges holding the printing frame to the baseboard may be loose.
Solution: Tighten, and try again.

Problem: The silk may not be taut enough over the printing frame.
Solution: Restretch the silk.

You Desire Unusual Textures and Special Effects.

Problem: To find materials and techniques to satisfy your needs.
Solution: Try makereadies on *top* of your baseboard and *under* the printing paper. These may be low relief collages of string, wire screen, leather, etc., pasted on cardboard. Experiment with other materials. Now, pull a print.

Using a syringe filled with china clay and glue, try making linear patterns on the screen. When dry, print in the usual fashion.

Brush, drip, or pour kerosene in areas on your silk screen. (These kerosene-soaked areas or linear patterns are the "positive" aspects of your screen. That is, *they* will pass color through to the printing paper). Cover the screen with glue, as you would for the tusche-resist method. The glue will "creep" away from the kerosene areas. When the glue is dry, you may print in the normal way.

Your Tusche Lines Print with Fuzzy Edges.

Problem: How to make tusche lines print in a more precise fashion.
Solution: Make a size composed of 1 teaspoonful of cornstarch to 1 cup of water. Sponge this size on the bottom of your screen and allow to dry. Then, apply your tusche in the usual manner.

You Wish to "Screen" Some Typewritten Words or Letters.

Problem: Is this possible? What materials will effect a solution?

Solution: Cut a mimeograph stencil on a typewriter. (It is also possible to draw on one with a stylus for certain results.) Affix the stencil with masking tape to the underside of the screen. Tape or block out the silk from the borders of the mimeograph stencil to the edges of your silk screen. Thin your ink or paint at the time when you are ready to print.

You Forget Which Solvent to Use for a Certain Medium.

Problem: How to avoid costly errors.
Solution: Consult the following chart; or, better yet, enlarge it and place it in a prominent position in your studio until there is no longer any need for it.

STENCILS, MEDIUMS, AND THEIR SOLVENTS

Acetate dope	Acetone
Enamels	Turpentine, benzine, kerosene
Glue (LePage's)	Water
Lacquer	Lacquer thinner
Litho crayon	Water—in drawing stage; mineral spirits, Varnolene, turps, or kerosene for wash-out
Nufilm, blufilm, profilm, etc.	Adhering solvent—acetone
Oils	Turpentine, benzine, kerosene
Photographic film stencils	Hot water
Shellac	Alcohol (denatured)
Tusche	Same as for litho crayon

The Margins of Your Print Begin to Show Paint or Ink Stains.

Problem: When screening large editions, paint may "creep" to the under side of your screen; paint may be too thin.
Solution: With a rag kept handy for just this purpose, wipe the bottom side of your screen from time to time; change and/or alter the consistency of your paint.

Certain Parts of the Print Do Not Screen Well.

Problem: Check the consistency of your paint or ink.

Solution: Remove the paint from the screen with a piece of cardboard; alter by adding the proper reducer, thinner, varnish, or whatever is required for that particular paint to improve its working characteristics. Pour the paint back in the screen and continue printing.

Problem: The impression lacks a certain sharpness.

Solution: On the assumption that a makeready does not remedy the situation, check the rubber blade of your squeegee. It may be rounded or otherwise marred. Resharpen the blade on garnet paper or the abrasive supplied by your local supplier for this purpose.

The Image Prints Double or Blurs During Screening.

Problem: The silk is not taut enough.

Solution: A makeready built up of tape applied close to the defective area on the under side of the screen may correct the difficulty. It not, the silk must be restretched.

Certain Areas of Your Print Develop Specks or Spots That Are Unwanted.

Problem: On the assumption that these spots are not caused by lint, there are pinholes in your stencil.

Solution: Hold the stencil up to the light. To stop these leaks in the stencil, touch a brush filled with the proper block out to each pinhole of light that is visible.

You Desire Gradated Colors in Certain Areas of Your Print.

Problem: How can you print several values of the same color or different colors so that they merge delicately from one to another? (This is normally employed for backgrounds).

Solution: Place a quantity of each of your selected colors in your screen in the desired sequence. Squeegee them across the screen simultaneously with a steady, straight motion.

After a few runs, you will obtain your desired results.

Your Printing Paper Sticks to the Screen after Each Print Is Pulled.

Problem: Besides possible smearing of prints, this slows the process of printing.

Solution: With pieces of cardboard, block up the hinges and the front of your printing frame. The silk will only contact the printing paper during the squeegee operation. It will snap off the print immediately. This is also a way to obtain sharper prints.

BIBLIOGRAPHY: THE SERIGRAPH

Arends, Jack, "Silk Screen Printing," *Design*, 41: 12–13, 23, March, 1940.

Biegeleisen, J. I., "Silk Screen Printing Process," *Art Instruction*, 2: 27–30, July, 1938.

Biegeleisen, J. I., *Silk Screen Stencil Craft as a Hobby*. New York: Harper & Bros., 1939. 139 pp.

Biegeleisen, J. I., and Busenbark, E. J., *The Silk Screen Printing Process*. New York: McGraw-Hill Book Co., 1941. 225 pp.

Biegeleisen, J. I., "Silk Screen Printing," *Design*, 42: 24–25, Jan., 1941.

Biegeleisen, J. I., and Cohen, M. A., *Silk Screen Stenciling as a Fine Art*. New York: McGraw-Hill Book Co., Inc., 1942. 179 pp.

Biegeleisen, J. I., "Silk Screen," *Design*, 43:9, June, 1942.

Kosloff, Albert, *Silk Screen Printing with Mimeograph type Stencils*. Chicago: The Author, 1946. 27 pp.

Kosloff, Albert, *Screen Process Printing*. Cincinnati: Signs of the Times Publishing Co., 1950. 194 pp.

Kosloff, Albert, *Mitography*. Milwaukee: The Bruce Publishing Co., 1952. 134 pp.

Kosloff, Albert, *Elementary Silk Screen Printing*. Chicago: Naz-dar Co., 1954. 42 l.

Leboit, Joe, "The Serigraph," *The New York Artist,* Vol. 1, No. 2, 12–13, 1940.

Mackenzie, F. W., editor, *Screen Process Printing.* Wealdstone, Middlesex: Skinner and Wilkinson, 1951.

Musser, Alice, "Silk Screen. A Device for Printing Color in Quantity," *Design,* 43: 18–19, Nov., 1942.

Shokler, Harry, *Artist's Manual for Silk Screen Printing.* New York: American Artists Group, 1946. 170 pp.

Stephenson, Jessie B., *From Old Stencils to Silk Screening: A Practical Guide.* New York: Charles Scribner's Sons, 1953. 239 pp.

Sternberg, Harry, *Silk Screen Color Printing.* New York: McGraw-Hill Book Co., Inc., 1942. 78 pp.

Strauss, Victor, *Modern Silk Screen Printing.* New York: The Pied Piper Press, 1949. 28 pp.

Summer, Harry, and Audrieth, Ralph M., *Handbook of the Silk Screen Printing Process.* New York: Arthur Brown and Bros., 1941. 64 pp.

Velonis, Anthony, "Silk Screen Process Prints," *Magazine of Art.* 33: 408–411, 481,, 1940.

Velonis, Anthony, *Technique of the Silk Screen Process.* New York: WPA Art Project, 1939. 35 pp.

Velonis, Anthony, *Technical Problems of the Artist.* New York: WPA Art Project, 1940. 15 pp.

Zigrosser, Carl, "Serigraph—A New Medium," *Print Collector's Quarterly,* 28: 442–477, Dec., 1941.

Appendix A:
Graphic Arts Supplies
and Sources

MATERIALS, TOOLS, AND EQUIPMENT FOR LITHOGRAPHY

AT THE OUTSET, it should be mentioned that substitutions in materials, tools, and equipment are encouraged. Each person will soon discover his own particular variations better to answer his needs. The following compilation represents a consensus.

Stones and Plates.

It is necessary to have at least two stones, and as many more as you can afford and store. I would recommend 16″ by 20″ and 20″ by 24″ stones for most beginners. They should be blue-grey or grey in color, and at least 3 to 4 inches thick. It may also be useful to obtain a thinner stone of about 20 by 24 inches for use as an ink slab, though a piece of plate glass of these same dimensions would also serve. A small 9″ by 12″ stone may also be purchased for use in graining. (See the section on Graining Materials.) Grained lithographic plates may be used as substitutes for stones. Although we have conducted experi-

ments with marble and other stones, the best results have still obtained from the qualitative limestones imported from Bavaria known in the craft simply as lithographic stones. Stones that are yellowlike in color are not recommended for most work. (27) *

Drawing Materials.

Korn lithographic crayons and pencils are standard fare in the medium of lithography. The pencils may be obtained in grades #oo (very soft) through #5 (copal—very hard). Softest is #oo, containing the most grease and therefore capable of producing

* Numbers in parentheses refer to list of suppliers on pp. 240–241.

the blackest black. For most work, it is suggested that you use #1 through #4. Lithographic crayons are boxed in dozens (the size and shape of Conte crayons) and are classified in the same manner as the pencils. (18)

Lithographs have been accomplished in the University of Southern California print workshop with such substitutes for Korn crayons and pencils as lipsticks, and hand soaps, children's drawing crayons, marking crayons, and, occasionally, homemade crayons based upon the formulae (with variations) of Senefelder, Brown, and others. (See Bibliography on Lithography for specific titles.) A list of necessary materials continues:

A stick of lithographic tusche (It is also sold in an expensive liquid form.) (18)

A crayon-holder or porte-crayon (if desired) (4)

A stick of Lithographic Rubbing Ink (18)

2 good watercolor brushes (sizes determined by your own work) (4)

Knife and assorted sharp implements (4)

Newsprint paper (18" by 24" pad is convenient) (3, 4, 32)

Nonwaxy or nonoily tracing paper (4)

Sketch book (4)

Conte crayon in stick or powdered form (sanguine) (4)

Lead pencils (hard) (4)

Steel square (4)

Drawing table or substitute (4)

Lithographer's needle or substitute (13, 23, 25, 27)

Assorted aids such as chamois skin, sandpaper, steel wool, silk, and various other devices for experimental work

Graining Materials.

Silicon carbide grain (carborundum) is the preferred graining material, though it is possible to use sand, pumice, flint, emery powder, ground glass, etc. It is suggested that you obtain carborundum in the following grades: Numbers 180, 220, F, and, if a very fine grain is desired, FF. (27)

A Levigator. This is a useful instrument for graining stones, if employed properly. The author owns one made of cast iron, $8\frac{1}{4}$ inches in diameter, and $2\frac{1}{8}$ inches thick. It has a free-turning wooden handle about 4 inches high mounted off-center on the cast iron base. The whole instrument weighs about 30 pounds. (Fig. I-1). The materials list continues:

A small lithographic stone (9" by 12") (27)

Graining stand or substitute (35)

Stone file or rasp (27)

Snake slips (Water-of-Ayr stones) (27)

Pumice stone (27)

Printing Materials.

1 lb. best black lithographic crayon ink (very stiff) (14, 16, 17, 25, 27, 30, 31)

1 ink knife or table knife (27)

1 spatula (27)

1 stone or plate glass inking slab (27)

1 lithographic hand leather roller (size to suit) (27)

1 lithographic hand composition roller (27)

1 pair leather cuffs for rollers (27)

1 pint each lithographic varnish (numbers 2, 5, and 7) (27)

5 lbs. gum arabic—crystals or powdered (The author prefers the former.) (27)

$\frac{1}{2}$ lb. phosphoric acid (13, 27)

1 lb. nitric acid (chemically pure) (13, 27)

1 3-ounce glass graduate (5, 8, 10, 27)

Several glass stirring rods or wooden paddles (1)

1 or more sponges (26, 33, 34)

1 white enamel household pan or substitute (34, 35)

½ lb. powdered resin (27)

½ lb. French chalk (27)

½ gallon turpentine (34)

1 medicine dropper (33)

Box of ordinary blackboard chalk (34)

1 3-inch rubberset brush (27)

1 lb. mutton tallow or substitute (27)

1 damp press or substitute (34, 35)

1 lithographic hand proving press, preferably geared (27)

1 can machine oil (34)

1 can grease (34)

19″ by 24″ white blotters (1)

Printing papers (see text) (2, 3, 13, 16, 17, 25, 28, 32)

Red press board, tympan paper, or substitute (27)

Scraper leather (27)

Wood scrapers (cut to fit your own stones) (27)

Rags (clean and soft) (35)

½ gallon kerosene (for composition roller) (34)

Lithographic crayon inks in colors (very stiff—your selection) (5, 8, 14, 25, 27)

MATERIALS, TOOLS, AND EQUIPMENT FOR INTAGLIO

Plates (5, 8, 13, 16, 17, 19, 24, 25).

Red engraver's copper (16- or 18-gauge)

Zinc (16- or 18-gauge)

Lucite, aluminum, magnesium, triple-metal, celluloid, etc., for experimental work

For Cleaning Plates.

Powdered whiting (27, 34)

Ammonia (35)

Vinegar (35)

Salt (35)

Grounds (8, 13, 16, 17, 19, 25).

1 ball etching ground (hard)

Liquid and powdered asphaltum

Soft ground, or stick of lithographic rubbing ink

Lump or powdered resin

For Smoking Traditional Grounds (13, 16, 17, 19, 25).

Hand vise

Coil of wax tapers

Tools for Working and Reworking the Image on the Plate (8, 13, 16, 17, 19, 23, 25).

Etching needle (or pin vise with appropriate needles)

Drypoint needle (or substitute)

Burins or gravers (numbers 2, 7, 9, and 12 are recommended)

Scoops or gouges ($\frac{1}{16}$, $\frac{1}{8}$, and $\frac{1}{4}$ inch are recommended)

Scraper

Anvil (34)

Hammer (for knocking up) (34)

Calipers (34)

Burnisher

Mezzotint rockers for grounding the plate

Mezzotint tools for patching the ground

Roulettes for mezzotint

Mezzotint scrapers

Sharpening Stones (34).
India oil stone
Arkansas stone

Abrasives and Polishing Powders (27).
Carborundum powder
Snake slips
Charcoal block
Emery cloth (numbers oo to oooo) (34)
Pumice powder
Rouge (34)
Schumaker brick
Tripoli (34)
Triumph polishing brick
Copper polish (35)

Acids and Materials Needed for Biting (33).
Nitric acid
Iron perchloride
Dutch mordant
Acetic acid
Tray for acid (glass, porcelain, certain plastics, etc.)
2 stop-out brushes (small and large) (13)
Stop-out varnish (13, 16, 17, 19, 25)
Liquid asphaltum (27)
Glass funnel

Equipment, Tools, and Materials for Printing.
1 professional-sized etching press (8, 13, 16, 17, 19, 25, 30, 31)
Heater (13, 16, 17, 19, 25, 30, 31, 34)
Jigger (35)
Ink slab (27, 34)
Etching ink
    Black S–134 Special (12)
    Black #514 (13)
    Your own mixture
Dry pigments
    Frankfort black, vine black, ivory black (11)
    Colored pigments (11)
1 pint burnt plate oil #oo (light) and #3 (heavy) (13)
Palette knife (4, 30, 31)
Ink dabber (employ a cast-off kid glove) (35)
Etching roller (composition—heat resistant) (13, 16, 17, 19)
Etching roller (leather covered) (13, 16, 17, 19)
Etching roller (rubber covered) (13, 16, 17, 19)
Damp box or tray for soaking paper (34, 35)
Wiping cloths (tarlatan, mosquito netting, cheesecloth) (9)
Etching blankets (white, woven felt 54 inches wide #6054) (7)
Papers (fine handmade printing papers preferred) (13, 28, 32)
Blotters (white 18″ by 24″) (1)
Turpentine (34)
Kerosene (34)
Denatured alcohol (34)

MATERIALS, TOOLS, AND EQUIPMENT FOR RELIEF PRINTS

The Block.
Hard, medium, or soft woods, (*woodcuts:* plank or side grain) (local)
Boxwood, maple (*wood engraving:* end grain) (15, 19)
Battleship linoleum (*linoleum cuts*) (local)
Plastics, masonite, wallboards, etc., for experimental work (local)

Materials.

Knife (4, 19, 23, 30, 31)

Assorted gouges and V tools (15, 19, 23)

India oil stone and Arkansas stone (34)

Machine oil (34)

Gravers and burins (assorted) (15, 19, 23)

Pen and India ink (35)

Carbon paper (35)

Pencil (35)

Printing Materials.

Brayer (5, 8, 19)

Block ink (5, 8, 19)

Papers (Japanese preferred) (28)

Tablespoon, baren, or other burnisher (35)

Press (4, 8, 19, 25, 30, 31)

MATERIALS, TOOLS, AND EQUIPMENT FOR SERIGRAPHY

Framing Supplies (5, 6, 10, 22, 26, 29).

Frame lumber (stocked 1⅜″ by 1¾″ or 1⅜″ by 2¾″)

Silk (stocked in widths from 40 to 60 inches; 6xx to 16xx)

Staple gun

Staples

Baseboard (should be several inches larger than the screen)

Roll of gummed kraft tape

Shellac, clear synthetic enamel, or acetate dope

1 pair of loose-pin hinges

4 angle irons

2 dozen 1″ screws

A 2″ or 3″ brush

Stencil Tools, Materials, and Supplies (5, 6, 10, 22, 26, 30).

A. Stop-out method

WaterSol or LePage's liquid glue

Brushes, syringes, hypo needles, etc.

B. Tusche method

3 watercolor brushes (small, medium, and large)

Tusche (sold in 2, 4, 8, and 16-ounce bottles) (18)

Le Page's liquid glue

Glycerine

Rags (clean) (35)

Pen and pencils (35)

C. Film stencil method (5, 6, 10, 22, 26, 29)

Film cutting knife, swivel knife, and assorted cutters

T-square, triangles, straight edges (assorted)

Scotch tape

Nufilm, Blufilm, etc. (Name is dependent upon brand carried by your supplier.)

Adhering liquid (for that particular brand)

Film solvent (for that particular brand)

Rags (clean) (35)

Lacquer screen filler

D. Photographic method: indirect (5, 6, 10, 22, 26, 29)

Kodapak acetate sheeting (clear or matte), Trace-O-Film (matte), Lustro Film (clear). Select one *if* you plan to make your own photo positive.

Photo stencil film (Kodak Ektagraph, Craftint, Dupont, Wetshot, etc.)

Scotch tape

A 3″ or 4″ camel's hair brush

Developer or sensitizer (for the brand selected)

Toughening and waterproofing solutions (if called for)

Solvents for removing stencil from silk (for the brand selected)

A #2 photo-flood lamp in a reflector (or an arc lamp)

Knife or razor blade

Small electric fan

Photographic vacuum printing frame

Large photo tray

Large piece of plate glass

Block-out dope

Blotters and newspapers

Paints and Mediums (5, 6, 10, 22, 26, 29).

Silk screen process paints, or artist's oil colors, or silk screen inks—or all three.

Mixing varnish

Transparent base

Extender base

Paint reducers or solvents: mineral spirits, kerosene, turps, etc.

Retarder

Overprint varnish

SOURCES FOR GRAPHIC ARTS SUPPLIES

1. American Camera and Photo
66 Randolph St.
Chicago, Ill.

2. H. Reeve Angel and Co.
7 Spruce St.
New York, N.Y.

3. Blake, Moffitt, and Towne
242 So. Los Angeles St.
Los Angeles 12, Calif.

4. Arthur Brown and Bros., Inc.
2 West 46th St.
New York 36, N.Y.

5. California Ink Co.
2939 East Pico Blvd.
Los Angeles 23, Calif.

6. Colonial Process Supply Co.
140 West 23rd St.
New York 11, N.Y.

7. Continental Felt Co.
22–26 West 15th St.
New York 11, N.Y.

8. Craftools, Inc.
396 Broadway
New York 13, N.Y.

9. Dazians
730 Flower St.
Los Angeles 17, Calif.

10. Ernst Dorn Co.
2431 So. Broadway
Los Angeles 7, Calif.

11. Fezandie and Sperrle, Inc.
205 Fulton St.
New York 7, N.Y.

12. Gaetjens, Berger, and Wirth
35 York St.
Brooklyn, N.Y.

13. Graphic Chemical and Ink Co.
714 N. Ardmore Ave.
P.O. Box #27
Villa Park, Ill.

14. Chas. Hellmuth Printing Ink Corp.
1029 So. Kildare Ave.
Chicago 24, Ill.

15. J. Johnson, and Co.
4417 Douglaston Parkway
Douglaston 63, N.Y.

16. Kimbers Supplies Service
44 Clerkenwell Green
London, EC4, England

17. W. C. Kimber
25 Field St.
Kings Cross Road
London, WC1, England

18. William Korn, Inc.
260 West St.
New York 13, N.Y.

19. T. N. Lawrence and Son
2–4, Bleeding Heart Yard
Greville St., Hatton Garden
London EC1, England

20. Henry Lindenmeyr and Sons
    480 Canal St.
    New York, N.Y.
21. Alfred Metzger
    30 Irving Place
    New York 3, N.Y.
22. McLogan Sign Painter's Supply House
    1015 So. Figueroa St.
    Los Angeles 15, Calif.
23. Edward C. Muller
    61–3 Frankfort St.
    New York 38, N.Y.
24. National Steel and Copper
    700 So. Clinton St.
    Chicago, Ill.
25. Rembrandt Graphic Arts Co., Inc.
    Stockton, New Jersey
26. Screen Process Supplies Mfg. Co.
    508 West MacArthur Blvd.
    Oakland 9, Calif.
27. Senefelder Co., Inc.

69–20 48th Ave.
    Woodside, N.Y.
28. Stevens-Nelson Paper Co.
    109 East 31st St.
    New York, N.Y.
29. Underwood Supply Co.
    820 So. Hoover St.
    Los Angeles 5, Calif.
30. F. Weber and Co.
    1220 Buttonwood St.
    Philadelphia 23, Penna.
31. F. Weber and Co.
    705 Pine St.
    St. Louis 1, Mo.
32. Zellerbach Paper Co.
    4000 East Union Pacific Ave.
    Los Angeles 54, Calif.
33. Local pharmacy or chemical supply
    house
34. Local hardware store or paint supplier
35. Household, art, or homemade supplies

Appendix B:
Formulae and Recipes—
Old and New

MANY ARTISTS, at some time or other, seem to enjoy trading technical information with their contemporaries and/or gleaning "secrets" from their predecessors. While the former is quite a simple phenomenon to achieve as long as communication and good fellowship are free and unimpeded, the latter must be researched in a good print library.

The following notes provide a sampling of conversations, demonstrations, and some reading in the field of printmaking.

OTHER PRINTING METHODS IN LITHOGRAPHY

Method Employed by the Taller De Grafica Popular, Mexico City, D.F.

1. To 1 ounce of gum arabic * add 4 * drops of nitric acid. Mix well and spread with the hand. Blot with newsprint and fan dry.
2. Wash off acidulated gum with water.
3. Add turpentine and wash out the crayon and tusche, then sponge clean.
4. Roll up with black crayon ink.
   Sponge with water. Roll again until image is full strength.
5. Pull at least two proofs.
6. Re-ink stone and dry.
7. Tamp in resin all over the inked design. Remove excess with cotton.
8. Do the same with talc.
9. Snake slip the edges and make corrections.

* The gum arabic mixture is used in a thick, viscous state by this excellent group of printmakers.

10. Etch with 30 * drops of acid to one ounce of gum arabic. (Protect very delicate greys by first painting out with pure gum arabic.) Blot with newsprint and hands and thin to a very fine coat.
11. Leave overnight to dry.
12. Wash stone with water and regum with very fine thin coat. Fan dry.
13. Wash out with turps.
14. Sponge stone clean with water.
15. Roll up, and print edition.

Bolton Brown: My Personal Usage in Getting a Stone Ready to Print (1921).

Every drawing varies, of course; but assume an ordinary design drawn on grey stone with Korn's crayon, from which I desire to pull prints neither lighter nor darker, but just as it looks.

I will probably apply a layer of gum, working some water into it immediately with my hand. When thinned and evenly distributed, I pour on a little solvent naphtha, or turpentine, perhaps carrying a little kerosene or linseed oil—at the same time charging a dry woolen rag with the same.

With the rag I sop the crayon entirely off, then sluice the stone with much clean water, washing it finally with a clean cloth or sponge and water. I invented and domesticated this heresy.

The roller being now passed, the design now reappears, not doubtfully and with pain, but firmly and willingly. I do not overload it, but work on a water film that grows constantly thinner by evaporation. The tendency is for the stone to roll rather lighter as it gets dryer, the stopping-point being a question of judgment.

I fan the stone dry, dust on pulverized gum mastic, using my hand, brush off excess with a wad of cotton, apply talcum powder (French chalk) similarly, and am then ready to etch.

To as many drams of gum as there are units of 32 square inches in the stone, I add my acid in the proportion of 48 drops per liquid ounce. That is to say, if the stone has 224 square inches, I pour into my graduate 7 drams of gum ($224 \div 32 = 7$), to this adding 42 drops (from the dropper, or else 28 minims by measure) or acid † ($48 \div 8 = 6$; $6 \times 7 = 42$). This is well stirred. It is made fresh each time.

With brush or fingers, I apply a trifle along the edges and over the borders of the stone. If these need cleaning, I here grind them off with pumice, then give a similar quick thin coat of the etch all over the design. The mass of the etch still is held in the graduate. If stray specks exist or I desire to add lights, I quickly, through the wet film, cut or scrape them out. The stone is now as it is supposed to print.

I throw on the main body of the etch, instantly distributing it with a thin, flat, soft brush, several inches wide. A thick brush drinks up too much of the etch, and I am apt to dis-

---

* The acid quantities are for an average stone.
† The formula for the acid used by Bolton Brown is:
    3 ounces 65 percent nitric acid (chemically pure)
    10 ounces 33 percent muriatic acid (chemically pure)
    13 ounces distilled water.

courage even a thin one from doing this by wetting it a little to begin with. I brush the fluid about, sometimes favoring the design, until it no longer tastes sour; push the excess off the stone; and let it dry.

It may be printed at any time after a few hours, but it is safer if a few days are allowed.

Transfer Printing As Employed by T. E. Griffits.*

1. Transfer the drawing from paper to stone in the normal manner.
2. Gum and dry the stone.
3. Wash out stone with turpentine and *allow to dry.*
4. Roll up dry stone with a thin layer of ink. (Yes, it will black up entirely.)
5. Pour a 6-inch circle of gum over the stone; begin to clear stone by smearing cotton wads over the gummed surface.
6. When stone is somewhat clear, add a little water and continue wiping until stone is perfectly clean.
7. Damp the stone with a sponge and quickly ink.

Method of Albert W. Barker.

(This was Mr. Barker's method of printing a lithograph without an "etch.")

1. Pour gum arabic on the stone.
2. Let it stand, and delay evaporation by resting a sheet of glass a frac-

tion of an inch above the stone. (Rest the glass on tiny strips of cork.)
3. Tip up stone, and allow it to drain and dry.
4. Next day, wash out and roll up in the usual way.
5. Fan stone dry, and dust with talc. Again, gum down and allow to stand for several days.
6. Wash out and roll up lightly . . . Sponge freely with *magnesium chloride solution.†* Allow to soak for 5 to 10 minutes.
7. Finish rolling up. Use *magnesium chloride solution* throughout the entire printing instead of damping water.

The Author's "Basic" Technique.

This rather bald technique has been employed by the author in his beginning courses merely to convince the student that the lithographic process is direct, straightforward, and not overly difficult. Usually, at the first meeting of the class, a freshly grained stone is offered as the surface for a group "doodle." Everyone is urged to make some mark or line or form on the stone with litho crayon or tusche to see if and how it will print. The last person to work on the "doodle" is requested to "pull it together." Then, it is printed (in less than an hour) using the following technique:

---

* Mr. Griffits uses a second etch which follows quite closely the formulae of most other lithographers. It is his opening efforts that are unusual.

† Magnesium chloride should be added to the damping water so that, when measured with a hydrometer, the specific gravity of the mixture reads 1.0222 (about the specific gravity of sea water). Don't allow the chemistry to frighten you from trying this experimental approach. If you make too strong a mixture (because you have no equipment), all that happens is that your blacks do not ink up. The stone, however, is unhurt. Wash off thoroughly with water, dilute the mixture, and try again.

1. Etch.* Thin and dry the etch.
2. Sponge thoroughly with water.
3. Apply gum arabic. Thin and dry.
4. Sponge thoroughly with water.
5. Wash out with turpentine.
6. Wash stone with water. Go over with damped sponge.
7. Roll up and print.

SOME MORDANTS FOR VARIOUS METALS

A Formula for Aluminum Plates.

Potassium dichromate: 1 part by weight

Sulphuric acid: 1 part by weight

Hydrochloric acid: 1½ parts by weight

Add, in the order listed, to 10 parts of warm water

A Formula for Zinc Plates.

Chlorate of potassium: 2 parts

Hydrochloric acid: 10 parts

Add to 88 parts of water

A Formula for Stainless Steel Plates.

Iron trichloride (crystals) : 4 parts by weight

Grain alcohol (70%) : 1 part by weight

A Formula for Soft Steel Plates.

Hydrochloric acid: 1 part by weight

Nitric acid (chemically pure) : 10 parts by weight

Methylated alcohol (70%) : 5 parts by weight

Water: 35 parts by weight

A Formula for Copper.

Hydrochloric acid: 1 part by weight

Sulphuric acid: 1 part by weight

Potassium dichromate: 1 part by weight

Mix, in reverse order, with 10 parts of warm water.

MISCELLANEOUS NOTES OF INTEREST TO PRINTMAKERS

A Seventeenth-Century Formula for Making Aqua Fortis.

Though the chemical terms are obsolete, William Faithorne's recipe offers more than an academic curiosity:

Vinegar: 3 pints

Salt ammoniac: 6 ounces

Bay salt: 6 ounces

Vert de griz: 4 ounces

Put all of the ingredients into a large pot, stir with a stick, and bring to a boil several times. Cover the pot; remove it from the stove and allow it to cool. Pour the acid into glass bottles. Before using it, allow the mixture to stand for several days. If the acid is too strong, add a glass or two of vinegar.

---

* About 60 or more drops of nitric acid to 1½ ounces of gum arabic. Since editions are not pulled from these demonstration stones, the etch is not overly critical.

Some Solvents Employed by Artists.

Acetone, amyl acetate, amyl alcohol, benzol, butanol, butyl acetate, butyl lactate, carbon tetrachloride, diacetone, ether, ethyl acetate, ethyl alcohol (anhydrous), gasoline, gum turpentine, kerosene, methanol (anhydrous), mineral spirits, naphtha, toluol, wood turpentine, and xylol.

Some So-called Standard Sizes for Displaying Prints (Outside Dimensions).

14″ by 19″ or 14¼″ by 19¼″
18″ by 22″ or 16″ by 22″
20″ by 24″
22″ by 26″ or 22″ by 28″

An Excellent Manual on New Techniques in Fine Prints.

The Brooklyn Museum Bulletin, Vol. XIV, No. 1, Fall, 1952.

Making Your Own Transfer Paper.

Measure equal portions of fine dental plaster and household flour.

Make a soft, creamy paste of the plaster; add water from time to time and stir constantly for 15 to 20 minutes.

Make a similar paste of the flour; stir it into cold water and allow it to boil for about 5 minutes.

Add the plaster paste to the flour paste and boil for 1 minute.

Using a soft, wide brush, apply the mixture to a strong, qualitative sheet of paper. Two coats of sizing should be adequate. Hang the sheet from a line. When the transfer paper is dry, you may make your drawing upon it with lithographic crayon or tusche. Transfer the drawing in the usual manner.

Making Transfer Crayons for Relief Etching.

Melt in the following order:
White castile soap: 5 parts
Beeswax: 8 parts
Red shellac (dry): 4 parts
Lampblack: 3 parts

Bring to a boil for several minutes, then pour the molten mass into well-oiled molds. For those interested in experimenting with crayon making, see Senefelder's formulae and also consult Bolton Brown, *Lithography for Artists.*

Senefelder's Formulae for Lithographic Crayons.

	1	2	3	4	5	6	7	8
Wax	4	8	4	8	8	8	8	2
Soap	6	4	4	4	5	5	6	
Lampblack	2	2	2	2	3	3	3	2
Spermacetti			4	4				
Tallow						2	4	6
Mennig								2
Shellac					4	4		

Follow the procedure as given for making transfer crayons.

Senefelder's Transfer Ink.

Shellac: 3 parts
Wax: 1 part
Tallow: 6 parts
Mastic: 5 parts
Soap: 4 parts
Lampblack: 1 part

Mix all of the ingredients in a large pot with some water and bring to a boil. Stir the mixture constantly and allow the water to evaporate. Repeat this procedure. Filter the mass through a cloth, and store it in a dust-free vessel. To use, thin with water.

To Intensify a Color Ink when Printing a Lithograph.

Add tiny quantities of starch, water, and formic acid; add a drop or so of phosphoric acid.

To Keep Lithographic Ink from Skinning Over.

Cover the surface with dipentene before storing away; cover with water.

To Obtain a Clean Line when Cutting Curves with a Burin.

Lean the tool towards the outer edge of the arc as you swing the plate or block around.

To Prevent a Woodcut Gouge from "Slipping" along the Block.

Inspect the bevel on the cutting end of the gouge. Chances are it is too short. Resharpen the bevel and, this time, make it longer.

To Remove a Bruise from a Wood Block.

If you do not want the area of the bruise to print as a light surrounded by darkness, here is a method for levelling the surface once more: Lightly moisten the bruised area and pass a lighted match over it until the block regains its original height.

Lalanne's Doctrine for Intaglio Work.

"Lines which are to be deeply bitten ought to be kept apart from each other; those which are to be of medium depth ought to be nearer; and very shallow lines ought to be quite close to each other."

Blake's Transfer Method for Relief Printing.

With a mixture of gum arabic and soap, coat a sheet of paper.

Draw upon the paper with a brush filled with a mixture of asphaltum and resin in benzine.

Heat a clean plate, and place the drawing face down upon it. Pass through the etching press. Soak the back of the paper with water and peel the paper from the plate.

Add work, if necessary, with a brush and the asphaltum solution.

Bite the plate in a mordant made of two parts of water to one part of nitric acid for at least nine hours.

Print as a relief etching.

Tischbein's Ground (also Attributed to Johann Heinrich 1742–1808).

This approach is similar, in effect, to soft ground:

Tartaric acid crystals are crushed and dusted over a grounded plate *before* the ground has hardened.

The linear pattern is then drawn with a dulled point, employing some pressure.

Immerse the plate in the proper mordant. After biting, clean the ground off the plate and print in the normal manner.

The line quality will have an irregular, grainy look.

Senefelder's Hard Etching Ground.

Wax: 12 parts
Mastic: 6 parts
Asphalt: 4 parts
Resin: 2 parts
Tallow: 1 part

Melt all the ingredients in an iron pan until the asphalt is assimilated. Allow the mass to fire until one-third of the mixture has been consumed. Cool and shape as desired. Keep dust-free.

Making a Spirit Ground.

Gum dammar or resin: 2 parts by weight

Grain alcohol (70%): 4 parts by weight

Crush and dissolve the resin or dammar in alcohol. Shake the mixture frequently. After a few days, drain off the saturated solution and discard the residue. Use the liquid for coarse grounds. To obtain finer grounds, cut the liquid with pure alcohol. A few test samples on an old plate will determine proportions.

Substitute Grains for Aquatint.

Instead of resin, one may well employ any of the following substances alone or in combination:

Gilsonite powder (powdered asphaltum—hard)
Gum mastic
Gum dammar

Senefelder's Acid-proof Ink.

Linseed oil varnish (thick): 2 parts
Tallow: 4 parts
Venetian turpentine: 1 part
Wax: 1 part

Melt the ingredients in an iron pot and add lampblack (4 parts). Stir thoroughly. Allow to cool, then store in an airtight vessel.

To Make a Sulphur Tint.

To obtain washlike, tonal values on a plate, spread oil on the area to be bitten. Dust Flowers of Sulphur (powdered sulphur) on them. Though the plate will not be deeply bitten, it will print a flat, high-valued tone.

To Transfer a Detailed Line Pattern to a Plate for Engraving.

Coat a copper plate with gum arabic.

Trace the drawing onto the dry, gummed surface.
Lightly drypoint the design.
Wash off the gum with water and remove any burr present on the plate.
Proceed to engrave with your burin.

To Work a Plate in the Crayon or Chalk Manner.

Ground the etching plate with any hard ground.
Work the image with various roulettes, multiple needles, or other tools which will perforate holes in the ground.
Etch and print in the normal manner.
The result seems to resemble a crayon or litho drawing.

To Make Relief Blocks in Cast Lead.

This approach was developed in 1940 by the Hungarian artist, Bertalan Bodnar.
The design is worked in relief in sculptor's clay.
That which will print black is kept level.
That which will print white is built up in relief.
Molten lead is poured over the clay to produce a low-relief plate.
The lead plate is inked and printed as a relief block.

To Make a Cellocut.

Boris Margo, alone, deserves the credit both for inventing and bringing to high perfection this particular approach to fine prints.
A "varnish" (sheet celluloid dissolved in acetone) is applied to any flat surface (masonite, zinc, copper, wood, sandpaper, etc.).
Hills and valleys, delicate lines or jagged forms can be created by the

imaginative printmaker.

When dry, the new plate or block may be worked with woodcut or etching tools.

Further raised areas are added by using thicker solutions of "varnish."

Print as a relief block or intaglio, or both. The medium is flexible enough to be used in combination with other more usual approaches.

To Make "Plaster Prints" of Other Materials than Plaster of Paris.

The following materials make excellent substitutes for plaster of Paris:

Hydrocal
Cement
Magnesia
Dental plaster

To Obtain a Quick Working Proof without an Etching Press.

Rub lampblack into the intaglio lines of your plate.

Place a sheet of waxed paper over the plate and burnish the back of the paper quite thoroughly.

To Obtain a "Crackle" Effect in Serigraphy.

Mix and employ a glue stencil that is overly thick.

To Obtain a "Spatterlike" Effect in Serigraphy.

Deliberately employ a glue stencil that is overly thin.

Glossary

Acetic Acid. A mild acid used to clean the needled image on a grounded plate before biting in nitric acid or any other strong mordant.

A La Poupée. Intaglio process. A method of printing many colors simultaneously from one plate. Separate pads or rolled felts are used to ink and wipe each color.

Aquatint. Intaglio process. A tonal medium which permits "grainlike" values in the print ranging from silvery grey to intense black. A porous ground of resin or other substances is applied to the plate, heated, then etched a number of times to produce the required values.

Asphaltum. A stop-out varnish employed in the intaglio process when long bites are required. Usually mixed with turpentine or benzine for better control. Also one of the ingredients in hard ground. Also employed in lithography by some printmakers in preference to tusche. Called bitumen in older texts.

Baren. Usually associated with the printmaker of Japan. A slightly convex hand tool, about 5 inches in diameter, for burnishing the back of paper when printing from an inked relief block. Many Western artists use an ordinary household tablespoon for the same purpose, though the results are not necessarily equal in quality.

Bath. A glass, porcelain, plastic, or other acid-proof tray in which plates are etched or bitten.

Bench Hook. A "do-it-yourself" aid employed by some artists when cutting relief blocks. Keeps the block from slipping; allows both hands to be free. Made by fastening two cleats at opposite ends and opposite sides of a board.

Bevel. The sloping edge of a plate or stone.

Biting. The action of acid attacking metal—normally in a bath.

Biting Time. The length of time a plate has been or should be acted upon by acid in a bath.

Blanket. Felts used in printing an intaglio plate on an etching press. They are used in sets of three or more.

Blind Printing. A technique employed by printmakers to lend texture to a print. It is accomplished by running the print and a specially cut, *uninked* block through a press. Also referred to as gauffrage or *kara-zuri*.

Bordering Wax. Dental wax or its equivalent used to edge extra-large plates with acid-proof walls to allow for all-over biting.

Boxwood. The dense hardwood from the boxwood tree. Normally prepared in end-grain blocks for use in wood engraving. End-grain maple is a usable substitute for beginners.

Brayer. A felt, gelatin, leather, composition, or rubber-covered roller for inking blocks or plates. The leather-covered roller used for laying grounds in etching.

Bridge. A device used by some lithographers which allows close work while drawing, yet keeps the hands from touching the stone. A piece of wood with felt-covered cleats; a barrel stave.

Burin. Called a graver by some authorities; a hand tool with a half-round wooden handle from which projects a steel shaft sharpened to a square or lozenge section. Cutting edges of burins vary in size and shape. Used for engraving metal or end-grain wood.

Burn. In lithography, to use too much nitric acid in the gum arabic etch, which "burns" away delicate crayon effects.

Burnisher. A bone or metal highly polished, oval-sectioned hand tool which is used to diminish intaglio lines. Also refers to a baren or similar tool employed in the relief process.

Burr. The ridge of metal thrown up by the drypoint needle as it is drawn through a plate. Similar to the furrows of earth thrown up by a plough. It is the burr that creates the velvety line peculiar to the drypoint.

Calipers. A two-legged, pivoted tool used in etching for measuring areas to be corrected or for locating the area to be hammered up from the back of the plate.

Carborundum Powder. One of many abrasive powders which may be used for graining lithographic stones.

Charcoal Block. Engraver's charcoal in block form; used for polishing plates.

Charge. To cover or roll with printing ink.

Cliché Verre. Glass prints. Not a true print medium. Glass is "grounded" with a light-resistant coating. The artist needles his design through the ground, and prints are obtained on light-sensitive paper by photographic means.

Counterproof. The offset proof that obtains when a wet proof or print is placed upon a clean, damped sheet of paper and run through a press.

Crevé. Of great concern to etchers in the traditional mode: a segment of a plate that is incapable of holding a sufficient amount of ink to print properly. Lines laid too close together on the grounded plate may break down in a nitric bath and print grey instead of black.

Criblé. A technique in printmaking in which the pictorial effect is achieved through dots; tiny holes pierced in the wood block or plate.

Dabber. The traditional tool for inking a plate or laying a ground. Usually, it is a cotton pad covered either with silk or leather.

Damp Press. Any device or contrivance that allows paper to be properly damped for printing. An oilcloth, rubber, or zinc-lined covered box or its equal for damping paper.

Deep Etch. A deeply etched plate that allows for relief and intaglio color printing simultaneously; also refers to some of Blake's work, plates by Posada, and others more experimental in approach.

Diamond Point. A diamond-tipped drypoint needle set in a convenient, comfortable-feeling handle. Other points useful as drypoint needles include steel, ruby, or sapphire.

Drypoint. Intaglio process. A medium whose prime characteristic is a soft, warm, velvety line. The burr, which is responsible for this line, breaks down after repeated printing.

Dust Bag. A bag of silk, nylon, or other finely woven fabric containing powdered resin for use in aquatint.

Dust Box. A light-weight, airtight box employed to ground plates with resin dust for the aquatint process.

Dusting. The act of applying powdered resin onto the surface of a plate in aquatinting.

Dutch Mordant. A mixture of potassium chlorate with hydrochloric acid used for fine biting.

Échoppe. An etching needle ground to an oblique face; used by Callot to obtain swelling lines reminiscent of engraving.

End Grain. A block of wood in which the grain runs perpendicular to the surface; especially prepared for wood engraving. Woodcuts are made on the plank grain.

Engraver's Pad. A circular, convex, sand-filled leather-covered pad on which some engravers rest their plates while engraving.

Engraving. Intaglio process: the act of driving a burin or graver through a plate. Relief process: to incise lines in an end-grain block of wood. Also refers to the print obtained from an engraved plate or a block of wood. When loosely used, covers all prints which utilize a press.

Etching. Intaglio process. Biting a plate with acid through the needled image on a ground in order to obtain that image on paper. Also refers to the print obtained from an etched plate.

Etching Ground. See GROUND.

Etching Needle. A blunt, rounded steel point used to lay open the ground on an etching plate.

Etching Press. A press for printing etchings and all other intaglio plates. It operates on a principle similar to that of a clotheswringer.

Extender. A mixing white used in serigraphy to add body to the paint and increase coverage.

Fatty Rag. An ink-charged rag that has been used repeatedly for wiping plates.

Feathering. A method of biting certain areas of a plate using drops of acid on the grounded surface and controlling this acid by means of a feather.

Flexible Shaft. A power tool similar to a dentist's drill; used successfully for engraving and textural effects. A variety of burrs and points may be employed in limitless ways.

Foul Biting. Accidental dots or irregular areas bitten into a plate. Caused by improper grounding.

Also referred to as PITTING.

Gauffrage. See BLIND PRINTING.

Ghost. The image of a previous lithograph that appears on the surface of a stone that is wet. Sometimes, despite a preliminary graining, the "ghost" still remains. Regrain the stone until it disappears.

Grain. Creating the drawing surface of a lithographic stone by grinding with an abrasive.

Graphic Arts. Ordinarily, refers to drawing or painting in any medium. In this book, the term is limited to include only those processes of hand printing that result in original prints.

Graver. See BURIN.

Grind. See GRAIN.

Ground. In etching, an acid-resistant, thin coating of beeswax, resin, and asphaltum (or like substances) rolled or dabbed on a metal plate. The design or image is scratched *through* the ground.

Hammer Up. Removing an unsuccessful area in an intaglio plate by hammering it up from the back, cutting away the surface with a scraper, and polishing or finishing it off with a burnisher.

Heater. A gas or electric hot plate with a solid flat top used to heat the intaglio plate before laying a ground. Also used to warm the plate before printing.

Heavy Etch. Used in lithography to describe a strong etch; a great deal of acid in the etch causing the stone to froth or effervesce immediately upon contact.

Impression. A print from an inked plate, block, or stone.

India Oil Stone. A sharpening stone used for burins, knives, scrapers, and other tools.

Ink Slab. A fairly large piece of plate glass, marble, or a lithographic stone on which prepared ink is rolled.

Intaglio. An incised or engraved design in a plate in one or more mediums.

Jigger. An inverted wooden box equal in height to the heater. Allows for ease in transferring warmed plates prior to inking.

Kara-zuri. See BLIND PRINTING.

Key Block or Plate. The block or plate that contains the master design from which all the color blocks and their registration obtain.

Knocking Up. See HAMMER UP.

Letterpress. The act or process of printing from type or relief blocks; the particular press used in this act or process.

Levigator. A 30-pound, cast iron, circular tool about 3 or 4 inches thick, with a handle mounted eccentrically; used to grain lithographic stones.

Lift Ground. A ground laid over an image previously drawn with a substance capable of swelling or lifting when the plate is soaked in water or acid.

Line Engraving. Refers to engravings in line accomplished with a burin on metal.

Linoleum Cut. Relief process. A block of battleship linoleum cut into with engraving tools, gouges, knives, etc., wherein the image to be printed is raised above the surface. Also a print from such a block.

Lithograph. Planographic process. A print or an impression produced by lithography.

Lithographic Crayon. Grease crayons (also in pencil form) with which one draws upon the stone. They vary in degrees of hardness and softness.

Lithographic Press. A press that works on a scraper principle used exclusively to print lithographs.

Lithographic Roller. A wooden-cored, flannel-wrapped, leather-covered roller used in printing lithographs. The leather cover is sewn on with the smooth side in.

Lithographic Stones. Imported limestone or other calcareous stone in slabs of varying dimensions, about 3 to 4 inches thick. The stones are hard but brittle, compact yet porous, and vary in color from a greyed yellow through grey to blue and blue-grey. (The darker the color the harder and more dense is the stone.)

Lithography. Planographic process. Prints are obtained from a stone on which an image has been drawn with greaselike substances. This surface phenomenon, after chemical treatment, operates on the antipathy between grease and water.

Lithotint. A technique in lithography wherein the image is created by means of washes of tusche.

Litho Varnish. Varnish used sparingly with litho ink to prepare the ink for printing. Also used for surface printing of intaglio plates when working in color.

Maculature. In intaglio printing, pulling a second proof from a plate without inking it again. A way of removing surplus ink from the lines and bitten areas.

Makeready. A device used by printers to clarify weak aspects of a design. Sheets of paper are laid beneath the plate or block, at certain places, until the correction is made.

Manière Noire. Working from dark to light, as in mezzotint. Also used to describe a tonal ground obtained by ruling a hardgrounded plate in at least four directions, and etching it.

Medium. An independent technique of expression such as etching, engraving, drypoint, lithography, serigraphy, woodcut, and so forth.

Metal Graphics. Invented by Rolf Nesch. He creates his printing plates by building them up with copper wire and other materials, then soldering them to the copper surface.

Mezzotint. Intaglio process. A medium in which the surface of a plate is methodically roughened with a rocker. Using various scrapers, the printmaker lightens certain passages, working from black to white, to clarify his design. Also a print obtained from a mezzotint plate.

Mitography. Another word advocated for serigraphy by Albert Kosloff.

Mixed Methods. A print obtained by combinations of mediums.

Monotype. An approach to art that lies between the fields of printmaking and painting. Results in one-of-a-kind end products. A method which involves working a design with oils or inks on the surface of a glass slab, metal plate or stone, then transfering the image to paper.

Mordant. Another term for acid used in biting metal plates.

Muller. A stone, glass, or metal block with an especially prepared surface used in grinding inks and pigments.

Mutton Tallow. Used to grease the scraper leather and the tympan in printing a lithograph.

Needle, Etching. The steel tool, or equivalent, used by the etcher to scribe his design upon the grounded plate.

Needle, Lithographer's. A sharp steel point encased in a wooden, pencil-like holder used to reduce accents on the stone when printing a lithograph. Also used as a tool to create white lines in tusche or heavy crayoned areas on a stone.

Nitric Acid. Used as a mordant in etching metal plates. Also added to gum arabic when etching a lithographic stone.

Perchloride of Iron. Used as a mordant for bitten plate work.

Pin Vise. An inexpensive, useful holder for phonograph needles and other points for use in printmaking.

Pitting. See FOUL BITING.

Plank Grain. Wood on which a woodcut is made; the grain runs parallel to the length of the block.

Planographic Prints. Prints obtained from a flat surface; lithographs.

Planographic Process. Surface printing wherein fine prints are obtained from a stone or plate. The image or design is neither raised nor lowered. Lithography is typical of the process.

Plate Mark. The telltale imprint of the edge of the plate left on all original intaglio prints; caused when wet paper and the plate pass through an etching press under considerable pressure.

Plate Oil. Burnt linseed oil used in making intaglio ink.

Plug. A wedge of wood forced into a block. Used by some printmakers for corrections, especially in wood engraving, woodcuts, or linoleum cuts. The faulty passage is cut out; a plug is wedged in its place, creating a new working surface.

Press. See LETTERPRESS, ETCHING PRESS, or LITHOGRAPHIC PRESS.

Proof. An impression obtained from an inked block, plate, stone, or screen to determine its particular state.

Proof, Trial or Artists Proof. A progress report, or early proof of a block, plate, stone, or screen.

Pull. The act of printing the print.

Register. The adjustment and readjustment of the separate plates, blocks, stones, or screens in color printing to assure proper alignment.

Register Marks. Tabs, crosses, triangles or other devices used in color printing for positioning the paper to obtain perfect register.

Relief Print. A print obtained from a relief block. Certain *collages* on cardboard may be inked and printed to produce relief prints. Also, metal plates may be printed as relief prints, in addition to their being printed in the intaglio manner.

Relief Process. See WOODCUT.

Remarque. Tiny sketches or trials drawn in the margins of intaglio plates; today, the artist works his image right up to the very edges of the plate.

Resin. When granulated, or merely crushed, used in the intaglio process as a ground for aquatint. Also used in the planographic process in powder form to strengthen the inked design on a stone before etching.

Repoussage. See HAMMER UP.

Retroussage. A method of obtaining luxuriant lines when printing from a bitten plate. After a normal wipe, a soft rag is lightly flicked over the lines to induce the ink to pull out of them slightly.

Rocker. The tool employed in mezzotint for laying a ground. A many-toothed, arclike, steel instrument with a handle in the center, literally rocked across the plate many times, in many directions, to produce an even textured burr.

Rotten Lines. Interrupted or fractured lines in etching, caused by uneven needle pressure on the grounded plate.

Roulette. A wheeled tool with a granulated head used to make dots or other perforations in a metal plate or ground.

Rubbing Ink. A rectangular cake of ink used in lithography to obtain soft tones. The finger, or a finger wrapped in silk or kid is stroked across the ink cake, and then applied to the stone.

Salt Aquatint. A method of obtaining a porous ground through sprinkling salt over a hot, thin-grounded plate. When cool, the plate is immersed in water, dissolving the salt.

Sandpaper Aquatint. An aquatint grain produced by running a normally grounded plate through the press with fine sandpaper face down upon it.

Scraper. A three-faced, hollow-ground hand tool with extremely sharp edges; used to remove metal burrs from the plate, to make corrections, or to incise heavy, deep lines.

Serigraphy. Stencil process. A method of producing original, multicolored prints having a real paint quality. Paint, ink, or other color is forced through a stencil of silk each time for each color required in the print.

Soft Ground. The addition of a non-hardening substance to hard ground. A medium within the intaglio process used alone or in conjunction with other mediums; allows grainy lines and limitless textures to be bitten into the plate.

Squeegee. A flat, wooden bar with a rubber blade. The tool used in serigraphy to pull paint across the screen when printing.

State. Each reworking of a plate constitutes a new state or stage of development of a particular print.

Stencil Process. A print method employing stencils. Serigraphy is one example.

Stone Rack. A homemade, wooden storage rack for stones, allowing them to be stored on end.

Stop-Out Varnish. A varnish employed in stopping out.

Stopping Out. Preventing certain lines or areas of a plate from biting, by brushing on an acid-proof material.

Struck off. Printed; pulled.

Sugar Aquatint. See LIFT GROUND. A sugar solution is used as the lifting agent.

Sulphur Aquatint. Used by Rembrandt and other experimental-minded etchers of the seventeenth century. Sulphur is dusted on oil-treated areas of the plate producing a grainy texture which, unfortunately, does not hold up for very many prints.

Tarlatan. Material used for wiping ink from the surface of an intaglio plate. Mosquito netting may be substituted.

Tint Tool. A type of graver used in wood engraving for making a series of delicate, parallel lines. The steel shaft is much thinner than that of the ordinary graver or burin.

Transparent Base. Aluminum stearate or similar substance used in serigraphy to reduce the opacity of color and improve screening, without affecting or changing the hue of the color.

Tusche. Grease in liquid form used in making lithographs and serigraphs.

Tympan. The tallow-covered sheet of red pressboard, zinc, or other material between the scraper of the lithographic press and the printing paper. A cushion.

Type-High. About three-fourths of an inch in height. The height of type in letterpress printing.

Washing Out. The act of removing crayon work from the stone with a spongeful or rag full of turpentine. This is done prior to rolling the stone with ink.

Water-Of-Ayr Stone. Also known as snake slip. An abrasive material in stick form. Used in lithography to clean the margins and edges of a stone. Also may be employed in the intaglio process to polish off scraper marks.

White Line. A technique of working up an image using a white line on a black ground.

Whiting. Used with water or ammonia in paste form to clean a plate before it is grounded.

Woodcut. Relief process. A block of plank grain wood cut into with a knife and various gouges, chisels, etc., wherein the image to be printed stands in relief above the rest of the block. A print from such a block.

Wood Engraving. Relief process. A block of end-grain wood cut into with burins, gravers, tint tools, etc.; a print from an end grain block.

Working Proof. A trial proof with additions and corrections indicated upon it. A guide for the next state of a print.

Xylography. Wood engraving.

Index of Artists and Prints

buscade," lithograph.

GINZEL, ROLAND. American (b. 1921), "The Significance of Integration," color linoleum cut.

GOLDSTEIN, MILTON. American (b. 1914), "Landscape," color intaglio.

GOUDIE, HARLAND. American (b. 1925), "Interior," intaglio.

GOYA, FRANCISCO. Spanish (1746–1828), "Disasters of War" Plate 30, etching.

GOYA, FRANCISCO. "Bravo Toro," lithograph.

GROPPER, WILLIAM. American (b. 1897), "Paul Bunyan," lithograph.

HAYTER, STANLEY WILLIAM. English (b. 1901), "L'Escoutay," color intaglio.

HELLER, JULES. American (b. 1919), "Farmer," lithograph.

HELLER, JULES. "Head," intaglio.

HOGARTH, WILLIAM. English (1697–1764), "The Cockpit," etching and engraving.

HOKUSAI, KATSUSHIKA. Japanese (1760–1849), "View of Fuji from Seven-Ri Beach" from The Thirty-Six Views of Fuji, color woodcut.

ISABEY, EUGÈNE. French (1803–1886), "Eglise Saint Jean, Thiers, Auvergne," lithograph.

JONES, JOHN PAUL. American (b. 1924), "Boundary," intaglio.

JONES, JOHN PAUL. "Presentation," intaglio.

KAHN, MAX. American (b. 1903), "The Blue Cat," color lithograph.

KANER, SAM. American (b. 1924), "Noel," deep etch and relief in color.

KNIGHT, DAME LAURA. English (b. 1877), "A Southern Blonde," mezzotint.

KOHN, MISCH. American (b. 1916), "Warrior Jagatai," wood engraving.

KOLLWITZ, KAETHE. German (1867–1945), "Stadtisches Obdach," lithograph.

KOLLWITZ, KAETHE. "Death Upon the Highway," lithograph.

KRISEL, HAROLD. American (b. 1920), "New Series #2," serigraph.

LANDON, EDWARD. American (b. 1911), "Northern Winter," serigraph.

LASANSKY, MAURICIO. American (b. 1914), "The Firebird," intaglio.

LAUTREC, HENRI DE TOULOUSE. French (1864–1901), "L'Estampe Originale," color lithograph.

LEJEUNE, PHILLIP. French (b. 1926), "Hercule et Omphale," serigraph.

MACCARI, MINO. Italian (b. 1898), "The Promoted," linoleum cut.

MACCOY, GUY. American (b. 1904), "Melon and Apples," serigraph.

MALTA, VINCENT. American (b. 1922), "Surrender," color intaglio.

MARGO, BORIS. American (b. 1901), "From Meteorites," cellocut.

MARK, HENRY. American (b. 1915), "Nocturne," serigraph.

McCONNELL, JAMES H. American (b. 1914), "Hammerhead Blues," serigraph.

MÉNDEZ, LEOPOLDO. Mexican School (b. 1893), "Homenaje al Heróico," wood engraving.

MOY, SEONG. American (b. 1921), "Yo-Yo Player," color woodcut.

MUENCH, JOHN. American (b. 1914), "Remnants," color lithograph.

PARIS, HAROLD. American (b. 1925), "Lament," lithograph.

PICASSO, PABLO. Spanish (b. 1881), "Dream and Lie of Franco," etching and lift ground.

PICASSO, PABLO. "The Ostrich" from Buffon's *Histoire Naturelle*, lift ground.

PIERCE, LEONA. American (b. 1922),

"Leap Frog," color woodcut.

PIRANESI, GIOVANNI BATTISTA. Italian (1720–1778), "The Prisons," Plate 6, etching.

POSADA, JOSE GUADALUPE. Mexican School (1851–1913), "The Jarabe Dance Beyond the Tomb," relief etching.

REDON, ODILON. French (1840–1916), "Yeux Clos," lithograph.

REMBRANDT VAN RYN. Dutch (1606–1669), "The Goldweigher's Field," etching.

RENOIR, AUGUSTE. French (1841–1919), "Seated Nude," soft ground etching.

ROBBINS, HULDA. American (b. 1910), "Beacon," serigraph.

ROGALSKI, WALTER. American (b. 1923), "Fiddlers," line engraving.

ROUAULT, GEORGES. French (b. 1871), "Grimacing Man" from *Flowers of Evil*, aquatint.

SCHANKER, LOUIS. American (b. 1903), "Birds in Flight," color woodcut.

SHOKLER, HARRY. American (b. 1896), "Netmenders," serigraph.

STERNBERG, HARRY. American (b. 1904), "All the News," intaglio.

TALLER DE GRAFICA POPULAR. Mexican School, 20th century, "Calaveras," linoleum engravings.

VIEILLARD, ROGER. French (b. 1907), "Sanson," line engraving.

VILLON, JACQUES. French (b. 1875), "After a Sculpture of Duchamp-Villon," etching.

WALD, SYLVIA. American (b. 1914), "Dark Wings," serigraph.

WAYNE, JUNE. American (b. 1918), "The Witnesses," lithograph.

WENGENROTH, STOW. American (b. 1906), "Meeting House," lithograph.

WHISTLER, JAMES A. McN. American (1834–1903), "Black Lion Wharf," etching.

INDEX

rubberset brush, 16
rubbing ink, 12
ruby point, 165

salt aquatint, 152, 153
sandpaper aquatint, 152
sandpaper, wet or dry, 91
sapphire point, 165
scalpel, 78
Schanker, Louis, 70
scorper, 86, 171
scraper, for intaglio, 143, 144, 179; for lithography, 24
scrive, 79
Senefelder, 1, 3; formulae for lithographic crayons, 246; formula for hard etching ground, 247
serigraph, making a, 207, 211, 212, 213, 216; planning a, 202, 203
serigraphy, definition of, 201, 202; stencils and mediums for, 231
shellac, 97, 206, 207, 231
shellac, glue- method, 217, 218; imitation method, 219
Shokler, Harry, 222
silk, 201, 203–207; stretching the, 205, 206
sizing, 193, 206
Smith, Charles, 97
soap, liquid, 161
soft ground, 153, 156, 157
soft steel, mordant for, 245
solvents, 246; for serigraphy, 231
sources for graphic arts supplies, 240, 241
spatula, 18
spirit ground, 248
"spit" biting, 132
spit-sticker, 86
squeegee, in intaglio, 137; in lithography, 17; in serigraphy, 206, 207
stainless steel, mordant for, 245
stapling machine, 203
steel, 125, 165, 172
steel point, 165
stencil, 217, 218; lacquer film, 218, 219; mimeograph, 230, 231; paper, 217; photographic, 219, 220
Sternberg, Harry, 117, 188, 201
stone, Arkansas, 171; carborundum, 171; India oil, 171
stop-out, in etching, 129; in lithography, 34; in serigraphy, 216, 217
sugar, saturated solution of, 161
sulphur tint, 248

sulphuric acid, 245
Swiss bolting cloth, 203
syringe, 222

taffeta, 203
talcum powder, 243
Taller de Grafica Popular, 242
tape, brown wrapping, 141, 203
tapers, wax, 126
tarlatan, 137
tartaric acid crystals, 247
Taylor, Baron, 38
tempera, 27
textiles, 74
tint tool, 86
Tischbein's ground, 247
transfer crayons, making, 246
transfer paper, making, 246
transfer relief printing, Blake's method of, 247
transparent base, 213
triplemetal, 125
turpentine, 20, 21, 127, 231
tusche, 12, 15, 33–35, 38, 44, 47, 48, 216
tusche-resist method, 216
tympan, 22, 24
type-high, 78, 85

Ukiyo-ye school, 63

varnish, lithographic, 19, 20
varnolene, 229
vaseline, 19, 80
vélo, 86
Velonis, Anthony, 201
vine black, 142
vinylite, 27
vise, hand, 126; pin, 129

Wald, Sylvia, 222
Warsager, Hyman, 201
washing out, 21
Washington press, 87
watch spring, 78
water, distilled, 243
watercolor, opaque, 219; transparent, 27
watersol, 211, 214
wax, 125, 126
Wayne, June, 47
Wengenroth, Stow, 47
Whistler, James A. McN., 113
whiting, powdered, 125, 194, 195
wire brush, 19

wire screen, 97

wood block, 78; removing bruise from, 247; substitutes for, 97, 98

woodcut, definition of, 74

wood engraving, definition of, 74; making a, 84–87

workshop solutions, to intaglio problems, 193–197; lithographic problems, 54–57; relief print problems, 98–99; serigraphic problems, 193–197

Wornowink, 213, 214

WPA Federal Arts Project, 200

Zigrosser, Carl, 201

zinc, a mordant for, 245

zinc-plate lithography, 36, 37